Reclamations

Essays on Culture, Mass-Culture and the Curriculum

PETER ABBS

Lecturer in Education, University of Sussex

HEINEMANN EDUCATIONAL BOOKS
LONDON

Heinemann Educational Books Ltd
22 Bedford Square, London WC1B 3HH
LONDON EDINBURGH MELBOURNE AUCKLAND
HONG KONG SINGAPORE KUALA LUMPUR NEW DELHI
IBADAN NAIROBI JOHANNESBURG
EXETER (NH) KINGSTON PORT OF SPAIN

First published 1979

ISBN 0 435 18024 X

Typeset in 11/12 pt Baskerville
by The Castlefield Press of High Wycombe,
and printed and bound in Great Britain by Biddles of Guildford

For Miranda

Contents

Acknowledgements

Parts of this book have previously appeared in *The Times Higher Education Supplement*, *Tract* and *Use of English*.

The opening essay 'Education and its Transformation' is an extended version of a lecture given at the Cockpit Arts Workshop for the conference 'The Arts and the Making of Meaning' (June 1978).

Introduction

The central aim of this book is not difficult to define. It seeks, in an educational context, to assert the reality and the importance of the inward world – the world of imagination, of feeling, of fantasy, dream, aspiration and vision. Since the time of the Renaissance there has been a marked tendency to ignore or even to deny the inner realm, and to confer reality only on the world of objects, of measurable quantities, of matter in motion. As I will try to show in this book, this major extroversion of psychic energy onto the outer has culminated in our highly technological society, where the machine has developed an exquisite refinement but where the inner self lies empty and neglected, perhaps more disregarded than at any previous point in history. Thousands of people in our society are, quite simply, estranged from the sources of their own being. In our times, the inner gods have become silent; primitive mythopoeic energies lie dangerously submerged. Like some long-lost piece of land, the inward realm stands in need of reclamation. The six essays gathered together in this book are an attempt at such a reclamation.

The difficulties facing such reclamation are formidable. We have not only lost touch with traditional methods for developing such inwardness; we are now, particularly in education, discarding the vital language of consciousness in favour of a mechanistic terminology and bureaucratic jargon. In educational discourse, prevailing concepts possess a delusive impersonality and seem more equipped to delineate the unambiguous movements of machines than the vulnerable and uncertain rhythms of individual consciousness. In general, the fate of such words as 'mythical' (to imply falsehood), 'subjective' (to imply prejudice) and 'fabulous' (now little more than a sloppy ejaculation) faithfully indicates the temper of the times, hostile alike to the deep expressive and the mythical dimensions of the personality. And yet the subterranean energies of the psyche do not disappear to meet the requirements of the dominant ideology. The danger, in fact, is that instead of being assimilated into daily life, conferring on it a depth and richness, the suppressed energies become cut off from reason and explode darkly in violent actions and indiscriminate mass-movements. There is no need to give examples here – the last four hundred years of our civilization are littered with examples of this savage, rational-irrational dialectic, and our own century has experienced the most extreme example of all. The cultivation of the inner life, the life of intelligent feeling and passionate enquiry, which is advocated in this book, labours against such a dissociation: it requires the prolonged and collaborative interchange of different energies in the psyche in order to fashion – the most difficult achievement of all – an intelligent and expressive union between reason and feeling, between the conscious and the unconscious, between light and darkness.

But how can the life of feeling be developed? How can the inward life be given shape, order and coherence? Traditionally, all the arts have been preoccupied with this question, not at the abstract level, but at the profound level of symbolic creation. The purpose of the arts was – and remains – to give the invisible realm of experience, so close yet so intangible, palpable symbolic form, in words, sounds, shapes, movements, colour. In fashioning a symbolic language for the inward experience of man, the arts not only promoted consciousness but also enhanced the life of feeling. Indeed, the importance of the arts in the origin and growth of inward consciousness cannot be overestimated. In their educational context, I believe that the arts are best conceived of as 'the expressive disciplines', and the first two essays in this volume set out to show the crucial value of these disciplines, and how in a curriculum preoccupied with cognitive understanding they have been woefully neglected.

Because our schools do not provide an expressive education, because they labour incessantly on convergent problems, seeking unproblematic results which can be mechanically assessed through a plethora of examinations, the suppressed life of feeling in adolescence surfaces elsewhere – in mass-culture. On analysis, a pattern of dissociation becomes apparent. On one side, we find the passive intellect and the acquisition of knowledge institutionally embodied in the school. On the other, feeling and its instant release embodied in the crude mass-produced forms of commercial culture. The dangers which attend such a dissociation and its posible outcome I have already hinted at. Knowledge without feeling becomes inert, a matter of indifference. Feeling without knowing becomes both blind and capricious, ready to attach itself uncritically to any powerful symbol, whatever its purpose, whatever its origin. The challenge posed by this sharp rift within the contemporary mind is enormous, and carries innumerable implications for teaching and teaching methods. Is it possible in our universities, colleges and schools to establish a form of teaching which heals the split? Is it possible to generate an educational process in which feeling and reason run together? Is it possible to bring together the conflicting elements of the psyche into a vigorous and sustained conversation, into dialogue? The middle section of the book grapples with these issues, and in particular explores the effects of mass-culture on the development of identity and considers, in the theory of mimesis, the two-way relationship between symbol and existence.

Certainly no answers to the many and difficult questions I have already raised can be substantial unless they provide philosophical premises and indicate necessary changes in practice. The last two essays of the book move in this direction. I make no special claims for my introductory essay on Existentialism. It is merely an attempt to open a door into a neglected subversive tradition of philosophical thinking which has been committed to inwardness and awareness, and has always recognized the power, even the primacy, of feeling in existence. At the end of the essay on Existentialism I consider some of the broad implications of Existentialist philosophy for the curriculum, and in the final essay, briefly and somewhat pessimistically, outline what I regard to be necessary but unlikely changes in our institutes of higher education.

Through all the essays runs a central strand: the need to recognize and to develop subjectivity. The intention is to reclaim the subjective dimension, to bring the neglected life of feeling and imagination into the educational process until the process itself becomes an expression of human wholeness. Of the five meanings for 'reclamation' given by the Shorter Oxford English Dictionary, the following four bear powerfully upon my theme:

1. The action of protesting; a protest.
2. The action of reclaiming from barbarism.
3. The making (of land) fit for cultivation.
4. The action of claiming the return of something taken away; a claim for something.

In the title of this book, I want both the negative and the positive associations to have full play. But, finally, I would like to feel that the prevailing note was positive. I would like to feel that the lost land reclaimed proves rich for cultivation, for new seeds, for a new, beautiful, and ultimately unpredictable, flowering of culture. And this against all the odds.

PETER ABBS
University of Sussex

On the Place of the Expressive Disciplines in Education

This condition of the two great departments of knowledge – the outward, cultivated exclusively on mechanical principles; the inward, finally abandoned, because, cultivated on such principles, it is found to yield no result, – sufficiently indicates the intellectual bias of our time, its all-pervading disposition towards that line of inquiry. In fact, an inward persuasion has long been diffusing itself, and now and then ever comes to utterance. That, except the external, there are no true sciences; that to the inward world (if there be any) our only conceivable road is through the outward; that, in short, what cannot be investigated and understood mechanically, cannot be investigated and understood at all.

THOMAS CARLYLE

To overcome the distortion of technics we must cultivate the inner and the subjective as our ancestors during the last three centuries cultivated the outer and objective.

LEWIS MUMFORD

ONE

Education and its Transformation

If the personality be once emptied of its subjectivity and come to what men call an objective condition, nothing can have any more effect on it.

NIETZSCHE

Emotion is the chief source of consciousness. There is no change from darkness to light or from inertia to movement without emotion.

JUNG

I

In this opening essay I want to defend the place of the expressive disciplines in education. I want to do this in a philosophical manner and on a broad front. We severely underestimate the power of philosophical ideas in this country, and try to turn the deficiency into a strength by elevating the tendency 'to muddle through' into a superior and exclusive way of life. In other periods, when there was more diversity and greater cultural wealth, such an attitude may have expressed an empirical good sense; in our own period, when the drive towards a collective uniformity is so relentless, when moral, existential and cultural confusion is so everywhere apparent, our fear of intellectual conception and philosophical argument is nothing less than a vice, for it is a habit which binds us, inexorably, to the accepting of an unacceptable status quo. Imaginative formulations, bold conceptions, incarnating the life of the mind, and making the life of the mind possible, are vital to the well-being of society and have the power to inaugurate fundamental as opposed to trivial, modish or merely bureaucratic change. It is true that social realities affect ideas, but the contrary is also the case: ideas have the power to affect realities, even to create them. I will not, then, apologize to my reader for the theoretical nature of my argument but perhaps at the outset I should make clear at least two of the terms I will use countless times. The first is the concept 'expressive disciplines': the second is the concept 'instrumentalism'.

By expressive disciplines I refer to the active teaching of the arts as a doing and as a making, as practice rather than theory. The disciplines of art, dance, drama, music, poetry, literature, film are *expressive*, because their distinguishing mark is that they seek to give personal form to actual or imaginative experience, an experience which is generally inspired by, or in some way impelled by, the power of emotion. The expressive disciplines are *disciplines* because the practice of the arts, quite simply, requires discipline; they require, for example, the habit of concentration, the living mastery of technique in intimate relationship to the nature of the experience being symbolized; and they also depend upon a delicate and developing discrimination, an endless process of selecting, discarding and refining. The arts require order and labour for their fulfilment. I think it is important to stress that the arts are not just a matter of release, of what is often called in the Freudian vocabulary 'discharge'. The word discipline denotes here the need to *work* within experience, and particularly within the elusive realm of emotion in order to realize it through symbolic form. I will return to this positive, life-enhancing conception of the expressive disciplines at the end of this essay, and explore it further in the essay that follows.

The second term I must briefly elucidate is 'instrumentalism'. I use this concept to denote the prevailing belief that the school is there as a 'tool', 'a mechanism', 'an instrument', simply to fit the child into the surrounding society, an institution to secure the adaptation of the child to his technocratic environment. The concept is a deterministic one, carries associations of Darwin's evolutionary theories, is held by many sociologists who frequently describe schools as units for socialization, and, for obvious reasons, is generally assumed by the political and commercial power-élites in any society.

Finally, I would like to point out that I am not going to be concerned with the similarities and differences between the expressive disciplines. What I am anxious to secure is a broad conception of education which would hold within itself not just a place for the expressive disciplines but a precise understanding of why they have such a crucial role in the development of consciousness. If we could establish such a conception – palpably establish it – then we would, I believe, be in the best position for securing a balanced and coherent curriculum in our schools.

II

Where an instrumental concept of life, and therefore an instrumental concept of education, prevails, the creative arts or what I prefer in their educational context to call the expressive disciplines, cannot thrive. Under the tyranny of instrumental views, the expressive disciplines not only get pushed out to the very edges of the curriculum (no more than one session of art, one session of music, one session of drama, one session of dance, per week in most of our Comprehensive schools), they even begin to lose their unique and defining characteristics. They become, as it were, corrupted by the dominant assumptions about man and education; in order to become accepted, they discard or modify their essential nature and begin to interpret themselves through alien categories. Let me give some examples. In the 50s, English teaching was defined by such pioneering spirits as Majorie Hourd, David Holbrook and Sybil Marshall as essentially an expressive discipline, a discipline committed to the sensitive articulation of individual consciousness through the immense energies harboured in the creative word. This movement, drawing on romantic and modern literature as well as on the disturbing problematical insights of psycho-analysis, has now been sadly eclipsed. A semi-linguistic, semi-sociological, semi-functional approach to English has blocked it out. The new tendencies, very much tendencies of the 70s, have culminated in a concept of English as 'skills' and 'communications'. The neutral vocabulary is significant. The emphasis on skills has turned grammar and punctuation into an end-in-itself – 'skills sessions' are now common in our classrooms, skills divorced from meaning, skills divorced from the need to utter, explore or convey experience – while the emphasis on 'communications' has thrown stress on the social and the public realm, and in so doing ignored the prior need of *expression*, the need to give authentic form to one's own experience, whether it 'communicates' or not. The expressive characteristics of English have thus been jettisoned, and the discipline has become either reduced to 'skills', dispersed as 'English across the curriculum', or diluted by being haphazardly mixed with 'social studies' and free-wheeling 'humanities courses'.

Over the last decade, a comparable change has taken place in drama. Among teachers of drama it would seem that the central concern has become 'social adaptation' rather than expression and realization of experience through the creation of symbolic form. Once again social function has come to the foreground and the personal and symbolic has been forced into the background. In his illuminating study *The Intelligence of Feeling*, Robert Witkin claimed:

> . . . a great many of the role-play situations improvised in drama sessions in schools have nothing whatever to do with drama although there is no doubt they are a good basis for practical sociology. The richness and imaginative wealth that we find in the young child we are loth to seek for in the adolescent . . . On the basis of what was observed and what was said in interviews it must be concluded that these drama teachers' concept of personal development was largely restricted to the notion of progressive social adjustment. Those to whom we spoke invariably invoked social adjustment as a justification of their educational role when they offered any kind of view of personal development.[1]

But, at least, even in its diminished and corrupted form (which may not be representative) drama still remains in our schools as *practice*, a doing and a making. This contrasts with the expressive discipline music, which has for the vast majority of pupils never emerged from the passive and the cognitive. Never, in fact, become expressive. For music on most time-tables in most schools refers not to the full-blooded generating of musical activity but to a rather sober period in which music is treated in essentially an historical and factual manner, the choir and orchestra (where they exist) being reserved for a tiny musical minority*.

*I have not given an example from the visual arts. Those interested in the way the visual arts can be corrupted by the instrumental ethic I would like to refer to an article 'On the teachability of Drawing' by Michael Daley published in the *Arts Review* (12 May 1978). In this article it becomes quite clear how the art of drawing has suffered by being interpreted through such inappropriate scientific categories as 'mode of inquiry', 'visual research', 'assembling of data'. In the reorganization of the Art Colleges, according to Michael Daley

> the artistically mindless forged an alliance with the mindlessly expansionist bureaucrats and convictions became the most dangerous liability. Far safer and institutionally wiser to substitute notions of art as 'research' into 'ongoing situations' than to stress the importance of learning how to mix colours on a palette or to draw a leg. 'Research' had the triple virtue of sounding progressive (and academic), being value-free, and being costly to implement. Drawing could only justify investment in pencils, paper, easels etc., but with research the possibilities

Under the instrumental imperative, one must expect the expressive disciplines to be in a continual state of insecurity, of neglect and of considerable confusion and demoralization. One must expect to find them always on the edges of meaning and never at its centre. Furthermore, as I have tried to show, there will always be a temptation for the expressive disciplines to redefine themselves in terms of the prevailing categories. In this way they may become more acceptable, but at the cost of losing their intrinsic identities. In the society at large, the arts can become in a similar way corrupted and compromised, technicized and commercialized. We do not have to look far for examples. Consider the state of architecture, the blank state of the visual arts, the bankruptcy of so many avant-garde manifestations.* The arts themselves, in their confusion, record the great crisis which technocracy engenders in culture. At such a time it is no easy matter to arrive at a fitting conception of the place of the expressive disciplines in education.

What is required – and the need is desperate – is a fitting concept of education, a concept which affirms the true importance of the arts and which generously includes them within the curriculum. In order to grope towards a true conception of education I must now take the argument through three stages.

In the first stage I will describe further the nature and destructive effects of instrumentalism.

In the second stage I will invoke, from our own Western tradition of philosophical thought, a conception of education fundamentally opposed to instrumentalism.

for spending – vacuum presses, cameras, video equipment, microscopes etc., were limitless.

Elsewhere in the article he asserts against the corrupted version of drawing: 'Drawings . . . are not quasi-scientific modes of research but full-blooded embodiments of artistic perception.

*Nearly ten years ago, in a lecture given four months before his death, Herbert Read, who had always been so ready to defend the new and the revolutionary in the arts, claimed 'Action Painting in the United States, Pop Art and Op Art have been *pseudo-movements* without stylisitic unity, without manifestos, without common action or association of any kind – *the creation of journalists* . . . ' In conclusion to his lecture he maintained 'Contemporary nihilism in art is simply a denial of art itself, a rejection of its social function. The refusal to recognize the limits of art is the reason why as critics we must withhold our approval from all those manifestations of permissiveness characterized by incoherence, insensibility, brutality and ironic detachment.' (my italics) The lecture *The Limits of Permissiveness* is reprinted in *The Black Rainbow* (Heinemann Educational Books, 1975).

In the third and last stage I will argue that even this valuable 'traditional' conception of education is quite inadequate. In an effort to recast it, to deepen it and broaden it, the place of the expressive disciplines in education will, I hope, become transparently clear.

I will move then, from prevailing thesis (instrumentalism) to antithesis to the transformation of that antithesis.

III

As Marcuse argued in *One Dimensional Man*, it is the inveterate habit of industrial society to think operationally. Transcendent and critical concepts are erased, and in the gaps functional definitions inserted. In industrial society, with the machine as its guiding and central metaphor, universal concepts – so vital to intellectual and cultural life – tend to be identified with the particular existing objects to which they may only partly refer. 'Democracy', to give a simple example, instead of referring to a principle and to different manifestations of that principle, comes to refer solely to the ballot box and the three-party system. The concept is made to denote the political system which already exists, and nothing else. Such practice makes it extremely difficult to think beyond the status quo, precisely because the concept has been robbed of its own subversive wealth. Like many twentieth-century writers, George Orwell was aware of the way in which language could be reshaped to prevent independent thinking. In *1984* Syme defends Newspeak in the following way:

> Don't you see the whole aim of Newspeak is to narrow the range of thought? In the end we shall make thoughtcrime literally impossible, because there will be no words in which to express it. Every concept that can ever be needed, will be expressed by exactly *one* word, with its meaning rigidly defined and all its subsidiary meanings rubbed out and forgotten. Already . . . we're not far from that point . . . . Every year fewer and fewer words and the range of consciousness always a little smaller.[2]

To make the point I am anxious to stress, however, it would be necessary slightly to revise Orwell's passage. The key sentence would then read: *Every concept that can ever be needed will be expressed by exactly one word, operationally defined and all its universal meanings rubbed out and forgotten*. If such a state was ever achieved a thinking beyond existing realities would be all but impossible because the major means of thought, language, having been deliberately and exclusively yoked to existing objects, would not allow, or rather support, such a movement. Each time the mind tried to escape, the corrupted symbolism would draw it back into its windowless cage.

Of course, such a narrowing of symbolism, such a literalism of the mind, does not only threaten philosophy,* or rather, philosophizing, it also destroys the creative arts which depend upon ambiguity, paradox, double-meaning, clusters of association, complexity of reference, all forms of counterpoint and contradiction. As the poet and painter David Jones claimed, 'The arts abhor any loppings off of meaning, or emptyings out, any lessening of the totality of connotation, any loss of recession and thickness through.'[3] A general impoverishment of symbolism entails a general impoverishment of all the arts.

Now it is painfully ironical yet entirely consistent with Marcuse's analysis that the current language of education is the language of operationalism, or what I defined at the beginning as instrumentalism. Education is now almost everywhere defined in terms of functions, markets, services, needs. Indeed, so much so that it is becoming an imaginative effort to think, feel and act in other terms. The instrumental concept of education is expressed, most obviously, in the Government's formulations

*It is, of course, central to my argument that philosophy itself has lost its transcendent qualities, at least in England and America. The philosopher no longer wishing to be thought a questor for meaning or a lover of wisdom has become in our century little more than a language technician. The redefinition of philosophy, making its pursuit one-dimensional, has severely curtailed its influence, as an active agency, upon society at a time when a hunger for existential meaning was never so great. Professor Blanchard describes the characteristics of modern philosophy as follows:

> The new philosophy is more intimately connected than the old with mathematics and natural science, and less intimately with literature, art, and religion; it sets comparatively little store by the history of philosophy, which, consisting largely of metaphysics, is chiefly a chronicle of confusion; and since it regards the search for a *summum bonum* as also confusion, ethics has turned its attention from the end of life either to reviewing the forms of behaviour or to analysing the language of our emotions about them. Among the qualities required of the philosopher those that used to be summed up under culture play a smaller role, while logical subtlety and acuteness play a larger role. This means in turn that philosophy is losing some part of that connotation of *wisdom* that it once carried.

(Lecture to British Academy quoted in Martin D'Arcy's *The Meeting of Love and Knowledge*). The last sentence forms a typical Anglo-Saxon understatement. The word wisdom is a positive embarrassment to one-dimensional philosophy.

on education: The following quotations are taken from the Green Paper *Education in Schools.*

> Education, *like any other public service*, is answerable to the society which it serves and which pays for it.[4] (my italics)

> The curriculum in many schools is not sufficiently matched to a life in modern industrial society.[5]

> It is vital to Britain's economic recovery and standard of living . . . *that the whole range of government policies, including education* contribute as much as possible to improving industrial performance and thereby increasing the national wealth.[6] (my italics)

The quotations reveal, quite starkly, the instrumental imperative. There is hardly need to point out that the expressive disciplines receive no proper attention, in fact barely a mention, in the educational document – for, given such a philosophy, how could they? It is also worth noticing how neatly education is absorbed into the status quo by being named 'a public service' (like sanitation, the Post Office, British Rail). Here, however, I want to show how such demands for industrial growth, further simplified in the daily running of our large Comprehensive schools, are turning all disciplines of enquiry into mere means for job qualifications. Under such pressure, education deteriorates to certification. And often the outcome is not only reductive but nonsensical. A large Comprehensive school I know of gives a pamphlet to each of its pupils at the end of the third year. In this pamphlet every subject has printed beneath it a list of jobs. (The equations at work here are simple. Subjects = jobs. The gaining of knowledge now = the gaining of money later. Educational Growth = Industrial Growth.) Even the nebulous field of Religious Education has its functions and, indeed, prospects. The list for Religious Education begins 'archivist, architect', runs on later to 'choirmaster and organist, cemetery and crematorium administration, funeral director', and concludes magnificently with 'stained glass design, teaching, woman church worker, deacons, etc.'*

*The complete list for R.E. is, in fact, as follows:
Archivist, Architect, Chaplains, hospitals, prisons, Services, Choirmaster and organist, Cemetery and crematorium administration, Funeral director, Minister of religion, Moral Welfare Worker, Missionary, Librarianship, Psychologist, Psychiatric social worker, Social work, Religious orders, Journalism, Stained glass design, Teaching, Woman church worker, deacons, etc.

Here operational rationality is taken to its ultimate absurdity, for how can 'religious education', with all its possible meanings and associations (of simplicity, poverty, renunciation, joy) deriving from the great religions, be a means to 'improving industrial performance'? Where there can be no positive clarification in line with government policy and the prevailing concept of education as mechanism to secure adaptation to environment, this school has decided on mystification, turning the grossest stupidities into the prevailing sanity. What we see, dramatically, in this example holds for all the other subjects and jobs listed. For disciplines of enquiry and exploration are, as I will suggest later, primarily symbolic forms of the mind in search of understanding, not steps leading up to the rotating doors of technocracy.

More generally, the instrumental view of education is recorded faithfully in the mechanical metaphors and grey abstractions of current educational discourse; in such words and phrases as:

> investment-process, stimulus, survival, strategic orientation, dynamic factors, feedback, through-put, in-put, contexted logistics, units, societal forces, ongoing interaction in interpersonal relationships, situational adjustment, mechanism, spin-off, institutionalised momentum, etc. etc.

Or again in such sentences as:

> the machine precludes aversive stimuli, provides immediate differential feedback, and often provides simultaneous multiple reinforcement of learning.

Or, as in the following suggested course for a new degree in education:

> In this course students will investigate the personality correlates of creative persons by psychometric techniques and then hypothesise motivational traits through an analysis of biographical material.

The effect of such language is to numb the mind. How is it possible to respond to it? How is it possible to think or feel when using it? It is a language which has successfully eradicated every trace of the individual in all his trembling actuality, in all his open vulnerability. It is not an accident that many of the metaphors, dead as they are, derive from mechanics (momentum, forces, factors), from military manoeuvres (logistics, strategy) and from behavioural psychology (stimulus, reinforcement). It is a language devoid of texture, resonance, depth, mood, and precludes style, that unique embodiment of distinctive thinking and focused feeling. The vocabulary of education resembles the mass artefacts of our time – the concrete office, the tower block, the motorway, the new housing estate, new shopping developments – in that it is thoroughly anonymous. Stare as we may, we cannot find ourselves reflected in it. It is the symbolism of a people in retreat from their own experience. It is the language of stasis, leaving education without a subject, without a history and without a future. It masquerades as a neutral language, but this it cannot be because in excluding man as the agent of his own education it is more than a little ideologically disposed. Its worst and deepest political effect is to seal off the interior world of consciousness and to label it 'unreal', or, in its own jargon, 'non-viable' – it thus obscures the source from which all great changes, all momentous renewals of the human spirit, come.

Here would be a good point to return to the expressive disciplines, because their very task is the development and refinement of inwardness through the creation of unique symbolic forms. But the argument I wish to make must be taken one step further before the importance of the arts within *a fitting concept of education* can be made clearly visible. What I wish to do now is to locate the antithesis to the prevailing thesis. To do this we do not have to move a single step. The antithesis slumbers in the great concept of education itself. We have only to stir the sleeper to find the meanings which transcend the instrumental imperative. The word education carries within itself a number of sublime meanings which have been deposited over the centuries, meanings which, if we can haul them to the surface, are intrinsically liberating, cannot be absorbed, cannot be nullified.

IV

The simple truth is that the word education can be made to serve the instrumentalist cause only through a sort of verbal bashing, a Newspeak reduction, for it is a word rich with layers of meaning, and resonant with diverse associations. Clearly the term education is broader than the term schooling, and need be in no way synonymous. It is quite in order to talk of busy schools in which *no education* takes place. It is quite intelligible to respond to the Green Paper *Education in Schools* by saying it unintentionally poses the question as to whether there can now be education in schools. Certainly, one of the enduring meanings curled up within the word 'education' derives from ancient Greece and concerns the power of simply asking questions, of questioning, not for its own sake, or in order to dissolve everything into a flood of doubt, but in order *to find out*, in order to come through to what would seem to be the case, whether in science, ethics, aesthetics, politics, religion or whatever.

Perhaps when we use the concept 'education' there lurks an image at the back of our minds of Socrates, whose habit of remorseless questioning (and listening, and questioning again) defined one of the first and finest forms of pedagogy. 'An unexamined life is not worth living', declared Socrates, and, as we know, his practice of relentless existential searching inspired his young student Plato as much as it alarmed the city-state of Athens. It is pertinent to my argument that Socrates was condemned for seducing the young into critical thought and for not honouring the traditional gods of the state. An instrumental conception of education, a conception in which all had to serve the interests of the status quo, rose up and, of course, successfully asserted itself against the impassioned rational concept of education as the *fearless enquiry into human meanings*, an enquiry which may have no outcome, no satisfying conclusion, no utility.

Socrates, one of the first great teachers in the long Western tradition, responsible for developing one of the abiding forms of pedagogy, saw his vocation as being a midwife to other men's conceptions; his task, as he experienced it, was to lead their thought out from the dark womb into the dazzling and open light of day. For Socrates, education was the sustained individual and collaborative probing of experience in order to find a provisional and constantly tested pattern of meaning for life, particularly moral meaning. Education was thus conceived of as an end in itself, *a formidable primary process of the mind in search of itself*. It needed, therefore, no justification outside itself, and if the state asserted claims counter to that of the individual consciousness then those claims had to be considered philosophically, and followed or modified or rejected accordingly. Education, the activity of questioning consciousness (in this tradition) does not necessarily contradict but always transcends the state and the status quo.

This habit of disinterested intellectual questioning (to be distinguished from scepticism) is one (among others) that we easily and actually associate with the word 'education'. Paradoxically, it is even invoked in the Green Paper *Education in Schools*. Of the aims given for schools, the first one moves in the wake of the Socratic concept: 'to help children develop lively enquiring minds; giving them the ability to question and to argue rationally . . . .' But the power to question with intellectual acuity and emotional seriousness cannot be circumscribed. It cannot be engendered with integrity where there are certain issues which are understood as *not* being open to critical examination. If a crucial part of education lies in the subtle art of questioning in order to find out, then all premises, at some stage, must be open to the shock of analysis and, where necessary, to radical reformulation. Following the spirit of Socrates, perhaps we should never talk about the educated man, but only of the man who is always in a state of educating himself, of being beyond the known and always setting up provisional camps on the fluctuating boundaries of the unknown.

Robert Cushman in his study of Plato's philosophy described the Socratic method of teaching, a method which dramatically enacts his conception of education as the unimpeded play of the rational mind over experience, as follows:

> The true pedagogue is a dialectician. In the first place, he knows how to induce "perplexity" where ignorance is joined with conceit of knowledge. By plying the mind of his pupil with appropriate questions, he invites a reconsideration of conventional and engrafted opinion. He engages in "joint-inquiry" with his pupil. He does not prematurely intrude solutions. He solicits response and cross-examines each answer with a view to its implications. In this way he clears up the false assumptions of deposited opinion. He opens a path for the mind to move gradually in the direction of truth, which is the objective of its native propensity. By letting the discussion have its head, being sure to divide and classify things according to their real similarities and differences, the teacher helps to dispose the learner's mind in the direction of reality so that the latter may discern for himself.[7]

The Socratic concept of education, as collaborative, sustained, rational enquiry into meaning (with the necessary discarding of mere opinion) was one of the sublime achievements of Greek culture, and I will have reason to return to it in a later essay in this book. The conception became part of the European humanist tradition – it permeated much of the nineteenth-century debate on education. It can be found surfacing in the works of such diverse and influential writers as Matthew Arnold, who often invoked 'the free play of mind over experience', and John Stuart Mill, who maintained 'better Socrates unsatisfied than a pig satisfied'; in Cardinal Newman, whose concept of a Liberal Education was 'simply the cultivation of the intellect, as such, and its object is nothing more or less than intellectual excellence' and in John Ruskin, whose eloquent teachings have still to be recognized 'you must forget your money and every other material interest, and educate for education's sake only! or the very good you try to bestow will become venomous, and that and your money will be lost together'. And, of course, it runs through into our own century. What is R. S. Peters' assertion* 'education, then, can have no ends beyond itself. Its value derives from standards and principles implicit in it. To be educated is not to have arrived at a destination: it is to travel with a different view' but a reassertion of the Socratic concept?

In the rational concept of education as an end in itself we have drawn into the light the antithesis to instrumentalism. The prevailing thesis would have education serve society: its antithesis would have education serve transcendence – or, I would rather say, education, where it exists as actual activity, is transcendence. In the depth of the word we have discovered a rich deposit: a meaning which has endured, which can be mined and brought up to the surface and given further life in new contexts. Such a conception takes us way beyond the instrumental imperative.

V

Education as indivisible and self-justifying process – that is a key premise informing, from Plato to Peters, the rationalist tradition. I have indicated reasons for embracing it as a great and necessary premise. And yet, as interpreted by the rationalists,

*This assertion is made, of course, in R. S. Peters' influential lecture 'Education as Initiation'. As I will suggest later, the word 'initiation' strikes me as a good one, but it can and should be given meanings and associations which R. S. Peters' use would seem to rule out.

it is not only limited but dangerously inadequate. It is now time, in dialectical manner, briefly to scrutinize the rationalist tradition, with its exclusive emphasis on reason – in the next essay I will again advance, in greater detail, some of the arguments sketched here. The analysis will take us, fairly quickly, to an understanding of the expressive disciplines and of their place in education as an unfolding process of self-elaboration and understanding.

Any marked manifestation of the psyche tends to exclude its opposite. Here the dialectic method* is not to ask what is successfully embodied but rather what has been excluded. The task is to make visible all that has been left out. If we turn to rationalism, distancing what it asserts and exploring what it denies, we discover numerous repressed energies longing for release and realization. In the dark shadow of rationalism we find feeling and passion, fantasy and dream, the senses and bodily instincts, all neglected, all distorted because of this great neglect. Knowledge secured through the dreaming mind, knowledge secured through the imagination, knowledge secured through the senses, all these possible forms of knowing were contracted to rational knowledge, knowledge secured through ordered and tested propositions, with mathematics as their paradigm. This is an enormous simplification – Plato, for example, recognized the power of imagery to dramatize immense concepts, and was himself a master of imagery; he also paid homage to Eros and recognized the value of the arts in education – but it does, I think, accurately describe the dominant tendency of the rationalist tradition, a tendency which from the Renaissance onwards became all but monolithic practice. It is no accident that in our own age the dominant Anglo-American school of philosophy, which I will attack in a later essay in this book, employed the word 'emotive' to dismiss any personal judgement which could not be verified, and therefore in their view could not be discussed. Religious, aesthetic and moral insights, dilemmas and achievements were all classified as merely emotive (or 'private'), and could not be placed upon the philosophical counter for intelligent discussion. In fact, Logical Positivism was not a 'revolution' so much as the evolution of one strand of philosophical prejudice, centuries old.

*For a definition of the word 'dialectic' and a consideration of its various uses turn to the essay 'An Existential Approach to Education', pp. 104 and 105.

As James Hillman has shown in his indispensable book *Emotion*, the same prejudice informed much of twentieth-century psychology. In a chapter entitled 'Emotion as Disorder' he analyses numerous theories in which emotion has been conceived *as defect*. A few sentences quoted by Hillman will convey the nature of this characteristic and negative judgement:

> Emotion is a kind of malady which by its inner pressure produces in man agitation and irresolution . . . Strong emotions resemble madness.[8]
>
> (WOLFF)

> An emotion is an acute disturbance or upset of the individual.[9]
>
> (YOUNG)

> The conclusion to which I come is that they (the emotions) have absolutely no value at all, but represent a defect in human nature.[10]
>
> (HOWARD)

> In order to promote survival Nature would have been wiser to have endowed organisms with less emotion and more cunning and intelligence.[11]
>
> (CARR)

Freud himself, of course, adopted a shrewd but deeply negative attitude to the emotions. In his analysis of the passages, excerpts from which I have quoted, Hillman concludes, 'the disorder view of emotion uses a moral and ontological model the foundations of which lie deep in antiquity'.[12] With this interpretation we are thrown back again to the origins of the rationalist tradition, where the self came to be defined as intellect and where other forces in the psyche, which seemed to threaten or obscure the lucidity of intellect, were seen as being inessential. For Aristotle the unique characteristic of man, distinguishing him from the natural order, was not his mythopoeic imagination, not his powers of passion or his moods of ecstacy, depression, boredom, content, anxiety, through which he is destined to live, but his intellect, his ability to reason, to abstract and to classify. For Plato essential reality – Truth – could *only* be apprehended through the mind, which he called the pilot of the soul. Thus intellect and identity became virtually synonymous – and the passions often interpreted as threats to both. 'In fact', said Aristotle, 'one may venture on the broad statement that passion is not amenable to reason but only to force'.[13] In *Phaedrus* Plato demonstrated that conviction with disturbing ruthlessness, for in that work the dark horse (representing instinct), is not lovingly tamed, but lacerated into submission:

> The driver, however, experiences even more intensely what he experienced before; he falls back like a racing charioteer at the barrier, and with still more violent backward pull jerks the bit from between the teeth of the lustful horse, drenches his abusive tongue and jaws with blood, and forcing his legs and haunches against the ground reduces him to torment. Finally, after several repetitions of this treatment, the wicked horse abandons his lustful ways; meekly now he executes the wishes of his driver, and when he catches sight of the loved one is ready to die of fear.[14]

In the next essay I intend to examine in greater detail Plato's attitude to feeling and aesthetic education. But it must be clear how the above passage in its sadistic violence darkly hints at an emerging schizophrenia between mind and instinct which, as Nietzsche recognized, has been one of the marked pathologies of Western civilization.

Any marked manifestation of the mind tends to exclude its opposite. The placing of intellect at the centre of human existence threw the emotions out to the edge, and not only the emotions but the whole entangled mass of images, hunches, monologues, stray conceptual fragments and all that psychic flotsam which characterizes actual consciousness in its ordinary daily movements. It was thus almost inevitable that reason should culminate in a notion of pure objectivity which excluded subjectivity, leaving the self in all its muddled actuality unaccommodated and with few means for ordered growth. This development in which 'personal' is erased and 'public' inserted, is seen, for example, in R. S. Peters' essay 'The Education of the Emotions', which would have been more accurately entitled 'The Annihilation of the Emotions', for it reveals the rationalist tradittion on its inferior side, a tradition utterly incapable of comprehending the nature of its complementary opposite. What Peters' essay does is *not* to suggest coherent ways of educating the emotions but rather ways of making what is unique and personal common and public. Consider, for example, the following extract:

> One of the main tasks of the education of the emotions, beginning with the development of what Freud called the ego, which he connected with the sense of reality, must therefore consist in fostering the capacity for objectivity. This is not just a matter for ensuring

> that children are well informed; it is more importantly a matter of converting what natural curiosity children have into a concern for truth, and getting them to discipline themselves to submit what they think to public tests.[15]

The education of the emotions equals being well informed and submitting what one *thinks* to public tests! Extraordinary that a rationalist philosopher cannot see that he has advocated under the guise of 'education of the emotions' a thoroughly rational education! The philosopher has not comprehended but merely dissolved the emotions.* Elsewhere in the essay, the emotions, having been defined as forms of passivity, are linked with prejudices and their expression, significantly, defined as *methods of control, and canalisation*. Clearly the philosopher is in a state of white terror. 'There is finally', he writes, '*the problem of the discharge of passivity*'! But there is no 'problem', no 'discharge' and no 'passivity'! Once more we see how emotions are felt to be threats from within, defects of our human nature. Yet, Peters timidly warns us, with the insights of Freud behind him, and one must add, the same pessimism,** 'control can, of course, go too far'. In brief, Peters' essay is a major disaster. It italicizes that cardinal failure of the rationalist tradition to comprehend its balancing opposite – feeling.

Let me make explicit four points, two of which are implicit in my dialectical critique of rationalism so far.

1. Reason cannot comprehend the whole of the psyche of which it is a part, or, put in a more positive form, being is always more than we can conceptualize.†
2. Emotion, fantasy, imagination, dreaming, have their own characteristic forms, possibilities and meanings. They can only be comprehended from without if they have first been, in some way lived and 'known' from within.
3. A rational proposition can only materialize as action where

*It is also worth pointing out that the language R.S. Peters uses cannot begin to meet his subject-matter. It is impossible to write adequately about emotion with words like 'discharge' and 'mechanism'; it is equivalent to describing a kiss as 'a contraction of the lips directed at the other'.

**It is worth noting that the operational language, which we described earlier, reappears in R.S. Peters' essay. In the manner of Freud he talks about 'the *mechanism* of sublimation', at once a telling and a misleading metaphor.

†This is an existential proposition that I will explore in greater detail in the penultimate essay.

there is fitting emotion. Emotion gives knowledge motion. A proposition without emotion may be unquestionably true yet wholly impotent. Thus *any* serious philosophy must come to terms with the primacy of emotion.

4. Reason itself, particularly in its early stages of conceptualization, depends on the sensuous and the imagined. Our concepts of time and measure derive from the felt rhythms of the universe. Our number-concepts were first hand-and-finger concepts. Before the abstract idea there is always the prior life of rhythm and image, the creations of the dreamer, the artist, the poet, the musician and the dancer. As Herbert Read declared, 'First ikon, then idea'.

These four highly condensed assertions point in two directions. In one direction they point to the failure of the rationalist tradition to develop a comprehensive understanding of 'knowing' and 'being'. In the other direction they point us forward to new ground – where a proper appreciation of the place of the expressive disciplines in education can grow to maturity. They urge us not to deny the antithesis of *education as self-justifying process* but to transform our understanding of what that process entails. In locating the subjective realm of immediate and mood-dominated consciousness, with its interior images, interior conversations, silences, memories and anticipations, with its own bodily rhythms and sense-experience, we have come to the realm where the arts have their origin and their purpose. The question is: how can *these* energies be developed, refined, brought to pitch and meaning? We know, to some extent, how reason or abstract conception develops, and at what stages it can be promoted, because this has been the main concern of our intellectual traditions and the practice of our best schools. But what about, for example, feeling? How can feeling be developed, refined and understood? The question takes us beyond the rationalist tradition into territory we must reclaim and chart again.

Clearly, introspection provides one way of understanding feeling. Here, for example, is an excerpt from a diary of a sixteen-year-old girl, a diary kept at the suggestion of her English teacher and occasionally shown to him. The passage reveals a profound preoccupation with the *meaning* of feelings:

> Sometimes my emotions run riot with me and then I realise I am not mature enough to cope with my feelings. I have tried but I honestly

do not know what to do. *I cannot eliminate feelings that are in me, even if I do not want them.* I have kept a diary for a long time but for the last four months I have kept an exercise book in which I have recorded my attitudes toward people. I have not written in it every day, just when I have needed to write, and as I read through it now I notice how my feelings about certain people have developed. It has helped me tremendously, because even though on some days it is obvious I have misunderstood somebody, I can tell by what I write on a later date, that I have sorted it all out. I do not try to deliberately connect each piece I write. They are independent, yet time and again, I find I have either contradicted myself, or strengthened a point I made earlier. I know people think I am secretive but *I just prefer to take my time before I really commit myself. By writing exactly how I feel, I can try to understand myself.* Perhaps I sound conceited but I know I am very honest with myself. *I cannot pretend to have feelings when I have not.* Sometimes I have tried to pretend to feel the opposite of how I do actually feel, but it is useless. Automatically, a hidden person in me laughs and says, 'Come off it. You know you do care. Don't try to fool me'. Then I laugh, because it seems so funny to have *two people inside me, having such a good-natured disagreement.* The honest person in me always wins which can be painful sometimes.[16]* (my italics)

The young writer accepts the primacy of emotion – she cannot eliminate emotions she does not want, nor can she create emotions she would like to have – but, at the same time, endeavours to work within them in a positive but by no means uncritical manner. She enters into a relationship with her emotions, trying to see what they signify and trying to integrate them into her whole consciousness. The introspective habit generates a dialogue in the mind where opposing desires enter into a sustained conversation. Sometimes the conversation is good-humoured but at other points it is tense and urgent:

I suppose I ought to just realise how I am feeling and accept it, but how can I accept such destructive feelings as jealousy? Part of me says 'you do not let the jealousy out, so you do not really hurt anybody', but something deep inside me says, 'no I do not let it out. I do not hurt people with it, but it's destroying me. It's eating away inside me and it's making me feel bad'.[17]

*I am deeply grateful to Bernard Harrison for allowing me to quote from his as yet unpublished manuscript *What I Truly Feel*. It is perhaps also worth adding that Sandra's diary is constantly exploring the differences between inner and outer realities. She writes, 'I think the reason I cannot talk to a lot of people is because I have not got much of a social-self. Most people seem to have a social-self and a private-self, but I seem to be lacking in the first. Some people tend to consist mainly of a social self with a very small private self and this is not particularly satisfactory either.'

The experience is lived through; in this case, destructive feeling is not suppressed but explored and seen from different perspectives. *The thinking takes places within the feeling* and not outside it. In such a manner feeling is made intelligible without being negated. Feeling is brought into consciousness, its demonic energies, at best, enhancing and giving vitality to all that the self does.

Such naked introspection should be met with the greatest of sympathy and firm support wherever it emerges in educational contexts, but I am not sure that it can be, or should be, *deliberately* cultivated during adolescence. The possibility should be implicitly there for any student who wishes to take it, but, perhaps, not part of the visible curriculum. The general and more accessible way to the exploration of feeling and consciousness is through the expressive disciplines where the forms and procedures both protect and develop the exposed self. The concentration on symbolic form provides both distance (because the symbol is not the self) and intimacy (because the symbol yet expresses the identity of the maker). Because the arts work through symbolic forms, much of what is happening remains at an implicit level; the influences on the psyche are, therefore, often subterranean, seeping into the self without being consciously recorded, but nevertheless capable of effecting deep changes.

In the expressive disciplines it is possible to discern at least three patterns, three characteristic rhythms, although there is in practice considerable overlapping. These patterns all bear upon emotion and its integration into consciousness, and I wish to draw this essay to a conclusion by quickly delineating them in an extremely compressed manner.

The first rhythm or movement is from within outwards; a strong emotion within seeks immediate expression without; it desires form. The artefact made is thus the emotion in visible form. 'Dance', claimed Laban, 'is no static picture, no allegory but vibrant life itself'.[18] D. H. Lawrence celebrating his own form of poetry claimed 'The utterance is like a spasm, naked contact with all influences at once. It does not want to get anywhere. It just takes place. For such utterance any externally applied law would be mere shackles and death. The law must come new each time from within'.[19] The emphasis is not on form or technique but on spontaneous expression of the moment, this moment as experienced by this individual, unique and incomparable. The arts, in this particular pattern, are thus the immediate expressions of authentic consciousness. The feelings are developed by being expressed and given free movement. In my experience as an English teacher, I found children up to about the age of twelve tend to work in this manner – a spontaneous overflow of powerful feeling *un*recollected in tranquility – and tend to resist the notion of laborious reworking and refining.

The second pattern begins, as the first, with an emotion – but the emotion is not so insistent or so distinct. It is what we might call an ordinary emotion, vaguely there, largely submerged beneath the threshold of consciousness. Immediate expression of such an emotion would be inarticulate because it is in itself blurred, indistinct, less than real. A work of art could not materialize spontaneously from it. And yet it can be explored; the emotion, for example, might suggest a certain incomplete image, colour or rhythm, and these can be consciously developed. In this way, with an uncertain motion, a creative process can commence in which the actual making begins to free the emotion and define it. Bosanquet has described this pattern with admirable lucidity:

> In common life your sorrow is a more or less dull pain, and its object – what it is about – remains a thought associated with it. There is too apt to be no gain, no advance, no new depth of experience promoted by the connection. But if you have the power to draw out or give imaginative shape to the object and material of your sorrowful experience, then it *must* undergo a transformation. *The feeling is submitted to the laws of an object*. . . . The values of which the feeling is capable have now been drawn out and revealed as by cutting and setting a gem. When I say 'of which the feeling is capable', I only record the fact that the feeling has been thus developed . . . and the feeling as finally expressed is a new creation, not the simple pain . . . which was felt at first.[20]

The feeling is submitted to the laws of an object – how different this emphasis is from D. H. Lawrence's and Laban's – and in the process of submission to the making of a coherent artefact, the original feeling is transformed. In this pattern, we start with the ordinary self, move to the demanding creation of form and return to the self in a state of emotional transformation. The emphasis begins to fall on technique, on the object made, on the artefact. This interest in form begins to develop most noticeably with adolescents, probably because their emotions have become more complex, less clear and, at many points, quite problematic. I found, for example, many adolescents wanting two or three weeks actually to complete a highly wrought piece of writing.

The third movement may begin outside the self completely. Here, for example, an image or achetypal symbol or narrative holds within itself immense charges of feeling, and provides a potent framework for its expression. The following poem re-creates the crucifixion:

The Crucifixion

Blood and wood mingled in cruelty
Stained flesh puctured and torn and hung up like meat
A man's face, distorted in agony and despair
And hair lank and moist.

Naked limbs, streaked scarlet, and stretched
In the shape 'symbolizing suffering'
Men gazing, laughing, sneering,
'It's none of our business.'

A stiff, winced movement
Parched lips mould a stifled word
And form a broken sentence.
'Quick, give him vinegar.'

A rigid corpse, peace at last.
The crowd dwindle pathetically away.
They heard his words and saw him dead,
And they will crucify another day.[21]

(JANETTE)

As much of the emotion is clustered within the actual archetype, the writer is thus, in a way, drawing emotion into herself which she is then able to possess and make her own by a re-creation of that archetype. In this re-creation, much is given, the associations (blood, vinegar, wood), the sublime feelings, the dramatic significance, the narrative. It is thus more than an individual work, it is the personal re-creation of a central and communal masterpiece, enacting a recurring experience of the human race. Seonaid Robertson in her book *Rosegarden and Labyrinth* has shown how archetypes can be made the inspiring focus of art-lessons. But, of course, they are available for major use within all the expressive disciplines.*

In the first pattern we could say that the personal is given immediate form; in the second that the personal is developed through the form; in the third that the impersonal form itself releases the personal. Each pattern testifies to the way in which the expressive disciplines release, heighten, transmit, refine and explore the realm of feeling.** *We come to recognize and integrate feeling largely through the creation and contemplation of aesthetic form.* These patterns have important implications for pedagogy which, unfortunately, there is no time to explore here.

The expressive disciplines with all their diversities yet constitute one coherent symbolic form for the understanding and elaboration of life. It is thus vital that they should be strongly embodied in the curriculum, given the same weight in the secondary school as the humanities and the inductive and deductive sciences; given, that is to say, in simple quantitative terms, about one-third of any week for their pursuit. No one symbolic form gives final balance, but the curriculum as a whole should embody a fitting totality. Ernst Cassirer said of the various symbolic forms created by man in search of meaning, 'All these functions complete and complement one another. Each one opens a new horizon and shows us a new aspect of humanity.'[22]

There can be no balanced curriculum until the place of the expressive disciplines in that self-justifying process we name education has been fully appreciated and duly acted upon.

In conclusion, let me summarize the main thrust of my argument. I have suggested that we need to transform the antithesis to instrumentalism by bringing into the educational process new powerful elements, the elements of feeling, of imagining, of sensing, of dreaming, elements which were neglected, disparaged and, at points, denied by the rationalists and humanists. To bring in these elements and to insist without

* In *English for Diversity* I reproduce all the written work that came from exploring the crucifixion with a fifth form and a number of poems re-creating the resurrection.

**My analysis has concentrated on the neglected realm of feeling, but I would not like to leave the impression that the arts are concerned exclusively with feeling. They are concerned with a thinking and a sensing and an imagining *moved by feeling*. We can *know* the world through art – but the sort of knowing is not inductive or deductive but, rather, experiential.

apology on their crucial place in the educational process is to reclaim land that has been neglected too long. It demands that we go beyond the notion of education as 'initiation into public and differentiated modes of thought' by seeing education as also initiation into personal and differentiated modes of feeling, sensing, imagining and believing. It demands qualities that attend initiation ceremonies in primitive societies. It demands that 'public' is complemented by 'personal', that 'objective' is complemented by 'subjective', that 'fact' is complemented by 'fiction'. To insist on the elements of feeling, sensing and imagining as vital to educational process, is, implicitly, to insist on the place of the expressive disciplines, for these are the means through which these elements are given shape, order, differentiation and refinement. I have tried to suggest how through the characteristic patterns of creative experience in the arts this takes place.

The task before us, then, is twofold. First, we must insist on education as a noble end in itself, a quest for meaning and circumference. Secondly, we must insist on the crucial place of the expressive disciplines in that quest (and the next essay will try again to define the importance of the arts in the search for existential meaning). To insist on both is to insist on a gentle revolution. And, looking around at the state of affairs in education and more generally, I am inclined to think that nothing less will do, and that nothing will be more difficult to bring about.

TWO

On the Value and Neglect of the Expressive Disciplines in Education

The present theory of meaning assigns a firm place to the inarticulate meanings of experience and shows that it is the foundation of all meanings.

MARJORIE GRENE

Each human being swims within a sea of faint suggestive imagery. It is this web of pressures, currents and suggestions, something often so much less definite than pictures, which ties our fugitive present to our past and future, composing a globe of consciousness. We think with our body, with its yearnings and shrinkings and its ghostly walkings.

IRIS MURDOCH

I

The expressive arts in this country, as in all modern technocracies, lie on the very fringe of the school curriculum. One can be certain that each child in our schools will be frequently and formally exposed to the symbolic systems of mathematics, physics, chemistry, geography, history and literature, but there is no certainty that in the course of his school life he will be exposed in any systematic way to the expressive disciplines. There is no assurance that any child will master a musical instrument or learn to make music; there is no assurance that he will have experience of making plays or films; no assurance that he will have opportunities to write his own poems and songs; no certainty that he will have the chance to make pottery, tapestries, sculpture and so forth. It is true that the child will do some art – painting and drawing – but at Primary School this will probably be unguided and undemanding decoration or copying, and at the secondary level it will probably comprise one hour a week and become optional in the third or fourth year. Of course, there are exceptions, but I am seeking to describe the general pattern.

The Bullock Report pointed to the way in which in the Primary Schools drama becomes less important as the child gains in age:

Improvised Drama in Classes with 6 and 9 Year-Old Children*

	6 year-olds %	9 year-olds %
In class time only	38	43
In optional time only	14	5
In both class and optional time	33	11
Not at all	15	42

As can be seen from the above chart, it would seem that 42% of nine-year-olds do no drama in the classroom. If it was suddenly discovered that 42% of our children did no mathematics at nine, there would be a national outcry. But why is mathematics assumed to be of such importance and drama of so little consequence? Why are the expressive disciplines at the edge of the school curriculum?

Another way of looking at the problem is to consider the findings of the London Institute concerning the kinds of writing being done across the curriculum in sixty-five secondary schools:

	Transactional English %	Expressive English %	Poetic English %	Miscellaneous English %
Year 1	54	6	17	23
Year 3	57	6	23	14
Year 5	62	5	24	9
Year 7	84	4	7	5

I am not convinced by the classification system used by the Institute or the linguistic philosophy from which it derives, but if we understand transactional English to denote the recording of information (not allowing for personal response or personal interpretation), then we have further insight into the excessive emphasis on the factual and cognitive in our schools. That in

*I have reproduced the diagram as it is given in *The Bullock Report* although it can be seen that there is a slight discrepancy in the second column of figures adding up, as they do, to 101%.

the last year of the sixth form nearly *all* the writing (84% of it) is in the form of impersonal description is worthy of note, because it indicates infallibly the inexorable direction of the whole educational system. From a theoretical point of view we could describe our schools as embodying a concept of knowledge without knowers, of facts without feelings, of objects without subjects, and as such constituting an organized pathology of consciousness. The reality of schools deviates from this concept because in the actual classroom there is always a relationship; always, in fact, a human face to knowledge; always an irreducible existential element. Fortunately, these elements of subjectivity cannot be completely erased, but they can exist in differing degrees of strength, and it would seem to me that if we erect theories of knowledge which exclude the experiencing subject, then the elusive and intuitive elements in teaching will become insecure and hesitant, and thus the relationships in which all true teaching must be grounded, darkened and obscured.

II

Nietzsche claimed that in life 'we must enlist rather than resist those magnificent monsters, the passions'. I believe that our schools for the most part resist the passionate energies and engage at best, only certain parts of the human psyche, the passive intellect and the recording memory. Our schools are still based on an inert and outmoded concept of knowledge as facts 'out there' unsullied by the human consciousness. Thus education is still largely conceived as transmission of information from the teacher (as neutral medium) to the pupils, information which then has to be dutifully recorded by the learners and, through either writing, or verbal parroting, returned to the teacher. An objective process.

We need to examine this objective process in a wider context, because we can be fairly sure that if feelings are being rejected in one place as inapplicable they will emerge somewhere else, and that much more powerfully for being suppressed elsewhere. It is not in the nature of feelings to politely disappear when reasonably asked to. To get a little closer to this problem I would like to look at an excerpt from a short piece of autobiography written recently by an undergraduate at Sussex University. Looking back at herself as a young adolescent in school, she could recall becoming three distinct persons in response to the demands made by her environment.

She begins by making a few remarks about her secondary school:

> The Comprehensive I attended aped the Grammar School style. I was a prefect in the fifth year but had my badge removed in 'courtmartial' procedure during which all heads of department were present for absconding home to do some more valuable revision than was being done by the rote learning we were required to undergo as preparation for the History 'O' Level: Tests of twenty short answer questions on the names and dates of President Roosevelt's 'New Deal' Act, *no* discussion of what they meant or did!
>
> In a way I led three lives:
>
> 1. School girl – learning the facts – an exercise of memory only – not demanding although I found the subjects themselves interesting.
> 2. A more internal life – my imagination, private dreams, ambitions, working out of problems, analysing, thinking, intermittent diaries, painting, drawing, poetry (it still embarrasses me to mention this, but I think a lot of people do it). I read pseudo-psychological and sociological writing at a tender age e.g. "The Naked Ape" (serialised in the Sunday Mirror!) at 12 – a bad beginning I suppose but better than nothing. And "The Female Eunuch" at 14. I wandered round to the public library and read everything which appeared, to a fourteen year old, to be slightly risque! I also thought the "Sun" was O.K.
> 3. The teenager – this enveloped especially the playground gossip and changing-room giggles, the evenings at Richmond Hall (local bop – it was reggae at the time) and later the more 'sophisticated' (i.e. expensive!) disco-nightclubs. The "Alpha Z" was *the* place to go at the time. They all had space-age names, e.g. "The Intercon", "Cloud 9", "Zero 6". It sounded modern, and new, and exciting – another world.
>
> I seemed to be able to keep these roles separate. In fact you were forced to if you wanted to "succeed" academically.[23]

I have selected this passage because I am sure it is in many ways typical, though I suspect a large number of adolescents do not have access to the same sort of inner life. What we find here is, on the one side of her life, a drab and utilitarian education and, on the other, 'another world', of megatechnic noise and megatechnic celebration. It expresses perfectly the division I have been referring to. In fact our society not only expresses the division but houses it. School is for knowledge and the accumulation of knowledge. It points to work and production. Mass-culture (in the form of discos, for example) is for the simple and inchoate release of blocked emotion. It symbolizes leisure and consumption. The able adolescent must learn to live in both worlds and not confuse them. He must not become too passionate about learning, for it is an orderly and rational process, nor must be become too rational or critical of the bizarre dionysian pop-performers and their mindless antics.

In the second section of this book I will attempt to analyse the tremendous power and the formative influence of mass-culture on the lives of the young; here I would like to consider the other side of the dichtomy between passion and knowledge, between irrational subjectivity and inhuman objectivity. I want to address myself to the following question. Why have we developed a notion of knowledge, and therefore of education, which excludes passion, fantasy, intuition, feeling, hunch, apprehension, doubt, belief, impression, dream, vision and the symbolic forms through which these powers or states of being can be explored and elaborated, given form, structure and living coherence? To put the question another way, why have we evolved a notion of knowledge which takes no account of the knowledge of the poet, the artist, the composer, the dancer, for surely their symbolic forms are there for common inspection and represent ways of knowing and being-in-the-world? A brief historical answer to this question must be attempted. After that, I hope to return to the positive assertion in the last question – namely, to consider why the arts are so important, and how an initiation into their various languages could enhance man's life and suggest a way beyond the chilly imperialism of objectivity and technocracy.

III

In the West since the disintegration of the Medieval world-picture there have developed two powerfully dominant schools of philosophy, Continental Rationalism and Anglo-Saxon Empiricism Both, as I want now to suggest, because of their informing assumptions, could find no place for the various expressive cultural forms. Both schools developed a concept of knowledge in harmony with scientific exploration, and the innumerable discoveries and inventions of science seemed further to confirm the truth of the philosophical concepts. With the industrial revolution, which was, from this perspective, the social incarnation of these theories, the informing conceptions of the few slowly became the commonplaces of the many, so that today there is a widespread assumption that scientists and experts *know*, and that if problems are a matter of 'mere feelings' they are 'merely subjective', and that in life we should always look for 'hard facts' and be 'objective'. (We do not talk about 'hard' or 'solid' feelings, nor do we talk about 'mere' objectivity.)

In this context it is worth turning, first, to the Rationalist tradition. It was Kepler who lucidly gave expression to their faith in quantities and numbers. 'The mind', Kepler declared, 'has been formed to understand not all sorts of things, but quantities; the further a thing recedes from quantities the more darkness and error inheres in it.' Spinoza sought to understand man by reference to 'lines, planes and bodies'. Descartes, in his *A Discourse on Method*, tells us that 'I reckoned as well nigh false all that was only probable'. Behind this almost fanatical quest for absolute certainty was a mathematical concept of knowledge. Descartes writes:

> The long chains of simple and easy reasonings by means of which geometers are accustomed to reach the conclusions of their most difficult demonstrations had led me to imagine that all things, to the knowledge of which man is competent, are mutually connected in the same way.[24]

Descartes did not question the mathematical model. He assumed that what was or seemed logically necessary was also true in the sense that it also must refer us to truths about life. But the crucial point is that, given such an informing conception of knowledge, that truths can only be established through long chains of simple reasoning, then nearly all the main cultural forms slowly developed by man to find meaning and orientation in the world are relegated to a shadowy region. There is no aesthetics in Descartes' work, no philosophy of culture, nor could there be. It is interesting how in the opening autobiographical chapter of *A Discourse on Method* Descartes, examining his own education, maintains that history can never 'represent the truth', must always contain some fictions and exaggerations, and that poetry – in order, presumably, to make up for its lack of logical order – 'has its ravishing graces and delights'. Poetry, Descartes indicates, is concerned with 'the most agreeable fancies', and, having said so much, he quickly turns to mathematics, praising 'the evidence and certitude of their reasonings'. If, as the philosopher held, we can only arrive at the most important truths through the reasoned building up of clear ideas, then history, the study of past cultures, can have little value and *the arts no central place in the task of understanding, in the curriculum of the mind*. And yet Descartes did not stop to consider that the very clear thoughts he expounded might depend upon the languages he used, that such thoughts as 'cogito ergo sum' might be impossible in many languages, and that if such 'universal truths' could only be mediated through certain languages there might be a problem about their universality. His thinking was ahistorical, acultural, and constituted a flight from the human world. Inevitably it has had disastrous consequences for the human world and, particularly, for the arts.

Descartes' definition of the self makes, by all that it excludes, the general dilemma clear.

> I thence concluded that I was a substance whose whole essence or nature consists only in thinking and which, that it may exist, had need of no place, nor is dependent on any material thing; so that '*I*', that is to say, *the mind by which I am what I am*, is wholly distinct from the body, and is even more easily known than the latter.[25]

Given such an ontology, a concept of the self as pure mind, then there can be no place for the culture of the feelings or the culture of the senses, and, least of all, a place for the concept of wholeness, of heart and mind running harmoniously together.

The passage also reveals the rift which Descartes established in his philosophy between mind and matter: the mind as self stood on one side; on the other, the physical universe, including the body of man. On the physical side everything could be explained in terms of *matter* and *motion*. As with the wax he scrutinizes in *Meditations on the First Philosophy*, so with the world, all that is 'out there' is 'nothing, except something extended, flexible, and moveable', a world devoid of colour, taste, smell, texture and, at a different level, informing purpose. The primary qualities of the material universe are mechanical and mathematical. It was under this conception of nature that science made so many of its discoveries. The fact that the theory was practically productive made it seem infallible. The philosophy of mechanism prevailed, and tended to forget the problem of the cogito, the self locked in the machine.

In Descartes, in Galileo, Kepler and the great Renaissance scientists and philosophers, began that scientific revolution which cast into the darkest shadows the full symbolic energies of man. The traditional symbolism in which man and universe corresponded, in which the human form was also the form of nature (microcosm-macrocosm), in which life was regulated by the fixed stars and the fixed stars regulated by life, was slowly eroded. The traditional double vision turned into the modern single vision. Before the Renaissance many symbols had a double reference, scientific and spiritual, intellectual and emotional: what happened under the mechanistic theories of Descartes and Galileo was that much of the symbolism was taken over and the symbolic subjective element progressively eliminated. The symbols were reduced to signs possessing single unambiguous meanings which could be systematically used to chart the nature of the external world. There can be little doubt that under this revolution a truer picture of the universe developed. Relatively free from anthropomorphism, science thrived. At the same time this great advance in understanding of the outer tended to eclipse the inward world of consciousness. As a result, the inner came either to be understood in terms of the outer* or even denied.

The gradual effacing of all the symbolic images which man had thrown over the cosmos, giving it human order, drama and meaning, created in the most sensitive individuals an immediate sense of anguish, a feeling of deep loss. Pascal, a contemporary of Descartes, himself an important scientist, inventor, and mathematician, recorded this experience of cosmic loneliness again and again;

> Everywhere I see only infinities, which enclose me like an atom, like a shadow which lasts only an unreturning instant.[26]

> When I consider the short span of my life, absorbed in the eternity preceding, the eternity following, the little space I fill, and even that space I see swallowed up in the infinite immensity, of spaces I know not, which know not me, I am astonished and terrified to see mvself here rather than there, for there is no reason why it should be here rather than there, why now rather than then.[27]

*This tendency reached its peak, perhaps, in nineteenth-century materialism. Taine, for example, under the power of the scientific vision, could write 'vice and virtue are products just as sulphuric acid and sugar are' and 'today, history, like zoology, has found its science of anatomy'. Many of the humanities still yearn for the order of the natural sciences, an order which would seem quite out of keeping with the content of their disciplines.

The new space opened up by science left the individual surrounded by a Nature which had become morally indifferent to his fate and which was symbolically empty. Marjorie Grene, considering Galileo's conception of the universe (a conception very close to that of Descartes) wrote:

> It is not only poetry in the narrow sense, the craft of making verses, that is here exiled from reality, but the whole work of imagination: myth and metaphor, dream and prophecy. In the bare mathematical bones of nature there is truth, all else is illusion. Yet that 'all else' includes the very roots of our being, and we forget them at our peril.[28]

The passage can stand as our conclusion to this brief and inadequate study of Rationalism, for it is myth, metaphor, dream and prophecy* *and the state of mind which underlies them* that we would wish to restore to our impoverished state-school curriculum. If we are to do this we need a much broader framework than the Rationalist tradition can provide. Indeed, the narrowness of our curriculum is, I belicve, in part, an expression of the Empiricist tradition which I would now like to glance at.

The Empiricist tradition, while believing more in the inductive method and in the construction of our conception of the world through sense perception, was likewise committed to the remarkable advances of science. John Locke wrote in his influential *An Essay Concerning Human Understanding*:

> The commonwealth of learning is not at this time without master-builders, whose mighty designs, in advancing the sciences, will leave lasting monuments to the admiration of posterity: but every one must not hope to be a Boyle or a Sydenham; and in an age that produces such masters as the great Huygenius and the incomparable Mr. Newton, with some others of that strain, it is ambition enough to be employed as an under-labourer in clearing the ground a little, and removing some of the rubbish that lies in the way to knowledge.[29]

*According to Margaret Byard, 'By the end of the 17th Century the poet could no longer write with quite the same belief in himself as a prophet and seer into the nature of things; intuition had increasingly to give way to the revolution in scientific knowledge which was to follow.' (*Poetic Responses to the Copernican Revolution, Scientific American*. June 1977). Thomas Merriam in an unpublished article has argued that the Baroque movement was 'an immense effort to counteract the remoteness of the Deity implied by the mechanics of Kepler and Galileo. It took up the revitalization of symbols.' According to Merriam, the arts became, under the mechanistic theories, 'a subjective sentiment bereft of ontological support'.

The modest, meek and deferential tone towards science characterized the tradition of Empiricism, and is a measure of its philosophical position. The Oxford philosopher Quine, faithfully echoing this whole school of thought, recently announced that as far as he was concerned, philosophy and the philosophy of science were one and the same thing. It is easy and dangerous to over-simplify – but it would not seem a gross distortion to say that the Empirical tradition culminated in a very simple distinction which was applied with inexorable logic to every facet of life. The distinction was between a verifiable and an unverifiable utterance. If an utterance was verifiable, then it could be established by public and empirical procedure as being true or false. If it was unverifiable, it meant that there was no clear way of establishing and testing the evidence, and that it was either logically confused or emotive, a private judgement which one either liked or disliked. Aesthetic and cultural evaluations, like ethical evaluations, were seen to belong to the unverifiable category, and nothing meaningful could be said about them. The role of philosophy thus came to be that of analysis, of classifying and clarifying *and* cleansing. The philosopher became a language-technician, 'an under-labourer in clearing the ground a little and removing some of the rubbish that lies in the way to knowledge' – knowledge being defined as that which can be established by public scientific procedure.

With the Empirical tradition we find again a closed circle in which the language and experience of the expressive disciplines can find no entry. If aesthetics is a matter of private whim and fancy, and not also a mode of knowing, relating and existing, then the arts are impoverished and reduced to the level of wine-tasting, or, as Bentham actually implied, push-pin. And, as with the Rationalist tradition, we must also notice a philosophy which excludes not only feelings but also the whole confused mass of hunches, interpretations, intuitions, doubts, beliefs, fantasies which constitute our actual experience. The tradition of English Empiricism slices off nearly all the contents of consciousness and casts them into oblivion, leaving only a tiny segment which can be meaningfully analysed. In the third section of this book I will describe further, from an autobiographical perspective, the impoverishment of Anglo-Saxon Empiricism.

It was inevitable, then, that this tradition would inevitably ignore the expressive arts just as much as the Rationalist tradition.*

Some pertinent criticism of Empiricism came from within itself (although it went largely unheeded) in John Stuart Mill's *Autobiography* and in his essays on Coleridge and Bentham. In the latter essay his description of Bentham can be seen not only to focus on the limitations of the man but also of the philosophy he held:

> He had never been made alive to the unseen influences which were acting on himself, nor consequently on his fellow creatures. Other ages and other nations were a blank to him for purposes of instruction. He measured them by but one standard; their knowledge of facts, and their capability to take correct views of utility, and merge all other objects in it. . . . He saw accordingly in man little but what the vulgarest eye can see; recognised no diversities of character but such as he who runs may read. Knowing so little of human feelings, he knew still less of the influences by which those feelings are formed: all the more subtle workings both of the mind upon itself, and of external things upon the mind, escaped him; and no-one, probably, who, in a highly instructed age, ever attempted to give a rule to all human conduct, set out with a more limited conception either of the agencies by which human conduct *is*, or of those by which it *ought* to be influenced.[30]

Mill's autobiography marks a more personal attempt to transcend the limitations of Bentham's philosophy as understood and imposed on him by his father, James Mill. In the one remarkable chapter of an otherwise dry and fact-obsessed autobiography, Mill describes his attempt to transcend his own lopsided cognitive development. In that chapter, it will be remembered, he dramatically experiences the importance of the until then suppressed power of feeling. He discovers the necessary and complementary opposite so disregarded by the dominant school of English philosophers. Mill wrote:

> The maintenance of a due balance among the faculties now seemed to me of primary importance. The cultivation of the feelings became one of the cardinal points in my ethical and philosophical creed. And my thoughts and inclinations turned in an increasing degree towards whatever seemed capable of being instrumental to that object.[31]

*It is important to point out here that there has been a subversive tradition running through Western philosophy. The work of, for example, Pascal, Vico, Herder, Kierkegaard and Nietzsche records a fierce critique of pure Rationalism and Lockean Empiricism. It is heartening that these philosophers are now being read in some English universities. I will return to this subversive tradition in the last section of this book.

In Wordsworth's poems Mill found the integration of thought and feeling which he was in search of. But the meaning of this integration was never worked out in philosophical terms. Indeed, as Mill's own autobiography would seem to testify, the philosopher never achieved this integration himself, and so the English tradition of philosophy moved forwards unaltered by Mill's critical break-down, and all that it so obviously symbolized about the dissociation of thought and feeling.

Whether philosophy was conceived as the accumulation of well-tested and verified facts *or* as the application of mathematical logic in order to clarify the workings of the world, in both cases the expressive arts were accorded no value, and all the elusive qualities which make up our daily experience of life denied or undermined. The success of these schools of philosophy has, I believe, helped to secure an educational system such as ours which invariably places fact over feeling, object over subject, reason over imagination and seems incapable of labouring for their proper integration.* In the following passage from the philosopher David Hume the two schools can be seen coming lethally together, and all that does not meet their strict and simple criteria is thrown like so much offensive rubbish to the flames:

> When we run over libraries by these principles what havoc must we make? If we take in our hand any volume, of divinity or school metaphysics, for instance, let us ask, *does it contain any abstract reasoning concerning quantity or number*? No. *Does it contain any experimental reasoning concerning matter of fact and existence*? No. Commit it then to the flames for it can contain nothing but sophistry and illusion.[32] (my italics)

IV

We can find both the sources and the counterparts of Rationalism and Empiricism in Greek philosophy. Plato believed in the powers of mathematical reason. His ideal forms, existing outside nature, imperishable and perfect, possess the enduring

*Of course, there is nothing original in this point. Charles Dickens' brilliant polemical novel *Hard Times* shows how a hard, fact-centred philosophy in education destroys imagination and spontaneity of feeling. Indeed, the great Romantic protest, running from William Blake to D. H. Lawrence, can be partly understood as a revolt against Rationalism and Empiricism.

immobility of geometrical constructions. Aristotle, breaking away from Plato and establishing his own methods, laid the foundations of empirical science, continually insisting that every hypothesis be tested by all the available evidence and recognizing the need for constant collection and systematic classification. Yet, at the same time, both philosophers *were* concerned with the nature of the arts and the influence they exerted on human life. Neither of them doubted the attractive and dramatic energies of music, myth, drama, art or denied their power to order, change, enhance or degrade life. Both men were convinced that the arts could exert a formative influence on behaviour. In *The Laws* Plato even concerns himself with the particular rhythm with which the mother should rock the child – for good rhythm is harmony, and harmony (for Plato) is akin to moral goodness. Aristotle, for similar reasons, urges that music should be a vital part of the curriculum because 'music has a power of forming the character and should therefore be introduced into the education of the young'.

The most positive development of this theme is found in Book III of Plato's *Republic*. According to Herbert Read, author of the influential *Education Through Art*, some of the passages have concentrated within themselves all the crucial points in his own plea for an aesthetic approach to the curriculum. The following excerpt takes us to the heart of Plato's argument:

> SOCRATES
> 'Then beauty of style and harmony and grace and good rhythm depend on simplicity, – I mean the true simplicity of a rightly and nobly ordered mind and character, not that other simplicity which is only an euphemism for folly?'
> 'Very true', he replied.
> 'And if our youth are to do their work in life, must they not make these graces and harmonies their perpetual aim?'
> 'They must.'
> 'And surely the art of the painter and every other creative and constructive art are full of them – weaving, embroidery, architecture, and every kind of manufacture; also nature, animal and vegetable – in all of them there is grace or the absence of grace. And ugliness and discord and inharmonious motion are nearly allied to ill words and ill nature, as grace and harmony are the twin sisters of goodness and virtue, and bear their likeness.'[33]

Plato is here asserting that if we make the rhythmic arts the basis of education, then we develop in the young a sense of form and style, a grace in being, which is also the mark of moral goodness. In the subsequent elaboration of this key idea, Plato contends that such an education, such an active initiation into the forms of beauty, would also draw, imperceptibly, the young towards 'the beauty of reason'. Aesthetic education is the preparation for a wider education, leading out into rational understanding and moral goodness.

Two further points are worth making. Plato sees these harmonies of shape as not only characteristic of good culture but also characteristic of 'nature, animal and vegetable'. The symmetries of nature and the symmetries of art are in some intimate relationship with each other, as if there is in both man and nature an impelling function to seek form. The second point to notice is that Plato includes in his aesthetic education 'every kind of manufacture'. There is no divorce between art and manufacture, between aesthetics and practicalities. Good form is not only necessary for sculpture and art, but also for furniture, utensils, carpets, tools and machines – and the making of such objects is seen as an essential element of what Plato calls the 'true education of the inner being'.

Herbert Read in his book *Icon and Idea* contends that Plato's theory of art has been much misunderstood and misrepresented. To try and re-create the true nature of Plato's position he quotes in his reference notes R. C. Lodge, who in his *Plato's Theory of Art* argues that:

> The truly artistic life is not (as Plato sees it) a 'vita contemplativa'. It is not a life withdrawn from activity and concentrated upon perception or reflexion. It is the life which realizes in practice the ideals which it apprehends. The citizens of the model city are themselves the 'personae' of a drama which is, precisely, ideal community living. They live artistically. They project themselves into their roles. They make, each of them, an individual contribution to the integrated life of the whole. The general citizens, indeed, are living in a kind of dream-aura. They are all dreaming parts of one and the same dream. But their life is not a mere dream, forces of pleasure (as such), or wealth or power (as such). It is a dream which has a sense of guidance towards a final, ideal vision. This vision they are capable of apprehending (for the most part) only through art. They are helped by the music, the architecture, the marches and rituals which are an ever-present feature of their life.[34]

There is, of course, an attraction in the unified culture which Plato depicts. But it is, I believe, ultimately a false attraction. For all its strengths, Plato's philosophy of art is, ultimately, against man. I must now try to show why.

It is well known that Plato, in order to secure harmonious culture in his Republic, edited the great myths, cut out chunks of Homer, banished tales in which gods behaved immorally, and exiled, with some remorse but with no uncertainty, the free poet. Only a simple and austere art, its content in agreement with the good, was allowed. In brief, only a closed ritualistic symbolism was permitted. Such symbolism has the power of engendering a great sense of unity and solidarity, but it can very soon stifle the creative quick, the spontaneous energies groping for new forms and meanings. According to Lodge, the members of the cultured community 'were all dreaming parts of one and the same dream. It is a dream which has a sense of guidance towards a final, ideal vision.' There may be an important place for a settled and comparatively closed symbolism, and particularly so in the education of the young. But unless this symbolism is complemented by another mode of symbolizing which I will describe as personal and experiential, the society, and therefore the life of individuals within it, becomes frozen, confined to a set measure which can only be endlessly repeated. We need, in fact, to keep alive and vibrant two different elements in culture, one which is inherited and has something of the coherence Plato demanded, the other which is innovative, restless, seeking, even disruptive. They are in opposition but, like most opposites, they are in need of each other. Traditional culture provides the materials for innovative culture, but the two cultures gaze in opposite directions. Traditional culture is concerned with fidelity to the community and to the received traditions which make community possible. Innovative culture is concerned with fidelity to individual experience, that which is known, sensed, felt, apprehended from within. There must, I suspect, often be a war between these two cultures, and, if a living balance is to be sustained, neither side must win.

Plato had no room for innovative culture, yet without it his own culture would have quickly become a matter of barren repetition and lifeless ritual. For this reason alone Plato's aesthetic theory strikes me as inadequate. Plato sees art as imitation, never as exploration. It is interesting also to observe how having provided for the young such a broad education, he then insists on the severest specialization. The motto is 'one man plays one part only'. This specialism, a distinct element of modern technocracy, serves well the organized pyramid of power and control, but it would seem in sharp contrast with the broad education through art propounded in Book III.

Finally, we need to remember that Plato, like Descartes, saw the world built up by the senses as one of illusion, or second-order reality. Indeed, for Plato, the artist in portraying the world was at a third remove from the source of truth. What the senses perceive, taste, smell, touch, hear, is always imperfect, a shadowy copy of something beyond. Truth, as embodied in the ideal forms prior to materialization, archetypal and eternal, can only be reached through the operations of the unimpeded intellect. Above Plato's Academy was written 'A Credit in Mathematics Is Required', and one of his frequent remarks was 'God is always doing geometry'! In the end what the senses and the feelings revealed were inferior, parts of a dark realm, incapable of penetrating the real. Indeed, the arts, on his own argument, constituted only a preparation for the higher life of reason. *The reason is the true self* – as with Descartes. Perhaps, then, it is not surprising with the Renaissance and the revival of Greek learning and scholarship, that *the cultural themes* of Plato and Aristotle were discarded as superfluous. Plato had elevated the mathematical reason to the top floor in the house of consciousness. It was to this top floor that the Rationalists took their bags and scientific instruments. Why bother with second-order realities of culture, when the world was written in the clear and primary language of mathematics?

V

I will conclude by drawing together some of the positive conceptions about art which are implicit in my critique of Rationalism and Empiricism.

Throughout the analysis I have suggested the need for wholeness of being. I have criticized the dominant Western traditions of philosophy for excluding from their analysis the immense and rich complexity of actual experience. We are not pure minds, nor are we bundles of sense-perceptions. To insist that we are is to distort the nature of what is. Our experience is elusive, many-stranded, ever-changing, problematic, unfolding; it includes, often simultaneously, thought, feeling, imagination and sensation in one creative manifold. We are creative centres constructing a world we can inhabit out of a world which is terrifyingly dense and seemingly indifferent. Through the powers of symbolism, and particularly through the powers of language, we are able to grasp our own inner being and assert values, beliefs and aspirations. These are meaningful simply because they arise out of our existence in personal and endless attempts to clarify, to contain, to understand. The arts are valuable because they are an essential part of the existential quest for meaning, and because they keep sharp and subtle and various the tools necessary for the task.

Perhaps wholeness of being is the ethical goal which all aesthetic activity, consciously or unconsciously, moves towards, the artist desiring to confer on his own existence the unity he perceives in the best of his artefacts. Wholeness of being may have to remain, for the most part, a beckoning ideal, but if it is to be real and not counterfeit, it will have to include, in a tense balance, all the elements in the human psyche: thought, feelings, sensation, intuition, imagination and instinct. I would contend that the arts, because they actively engage, in one way or another, all these elements, are best equipped to contribute to the development of such an ideal. The arts do, sometimes quite dangerously, enlist the magnificent monsters of the passions, but they also enlist the constructive, cognitive and form-seeking energies of the mind.

It is precisely because the arts, by their very nature, bring into free play the various and conflicting powers of the psyche and seek a living unity between them that they merit a decisive place in the curriculum.

I would like to conclude with a few practical reflections. I argued earlier that society needs two types of culture, one hereditary, communal and somewhat static (like Plato's), the other innovative, immediate, personal and dynamic, and that both had to engage with each other, and that both, for the well-being of society, had to stand their ground. In our schools, alas, we have neither cultivated ritual and ceremony nor individual exploration and creation.

The word 'initiation' has been recently used to denote the nature of the true educational process. It is a good word, but those who have used it in educational circles have robbed the word of some of its more potent connotations (deriving from anthropology). We know from studies of primitive societies that initiation ceremonies are powerful, dramatic events in which the transformation of man from one level of being to another is demarcated and symbolized. Initiations are communal ceremonies with elaborate structures and symbols given. They mark important stages in the individual's life as it is seen by the community with all its complex and rotating needs. Dance, drama, singing, recitation, ritual are often all used to make palpable and real the transition from one stage of social existence to another.

In our own history, the Reformation and Industrialism were together directly responsible for destroying many of these festivities and rituals. Susanne Langer in *Philosophy in a New Key* points rightly to the general impoverishment of our symbolic environment. Reflecting on the work experiences of millions of people in factories (and, one might add, offices), she writes:

> This sort of activity is too poor, too empty for even the most ingenious mind to invest it with symbolic content. Work is no longer a sphere of ritual; so the nearest and surest source of mental satisfaction has dried up.[35]

And, looking beyond work to our general condition, she concludes:

> All old symbols are gone, and thousands of average lives offer no new materials to a creative imagination. This, rather than physical want, is the starvation that threatens the modern worker, the tyranny of the machine. The withdrawal of all natural means for expressing the unity of personal life is a major cause of the distraction, irreligion and unrest that mark the proletariat of all countries. Technical progress is putting man's freedom of mind in jeopardy.[36]

Schools alone cannot provide single answers to such enormous problems but they can develop ritualistic occasions, ceremonies which convey a sense of unfolding drama, a sense of a community giving symbolic form to its own deepest needs. The young are clearly attracted to football because it provides many ritualistic elements lacking in their lives. I am suggesting that these ritualistic elements should be incorporated into the life of schools and refined and deepened. At the back of my mind I have two images. One is of the Welsh Eisteddfodau, beginning in the smallest villages and moving up to the national celebration, with singing, harp-playing and recitation. The other image is of a class of thirteen-year-olds in a Steiner school giving a customary farewell to the single teacher who had taken them right through their primary schooling. I entered the hall quite by accident. It was dark because the curtains had been drawn. At the back a mass of candles on a large cake with many tiers were being lit. At the front, behind the curtains, there was the bustle of movement as the class prepared to make their various dramatic presentations to their teacher. And the hall itself was full of children, parents and teachers. The ceremony was expected to last a number of hours. In the new term the class would graduate to a higher level where they would be taught by many different teachers representing the specialized areas of human knowledge and an expanding adult community. What I had stumbled upon was an initiation rite, dramatic, ritualistic and communal.

Laban, whose influence was so decisive in developing the place of dance in education, argued eloquently for such rituals and festivities.* In his autobiography *Life for Dance* he claimed that:

> man's real purpose was to create a life with festive occasions; not festive in the sense of luxurious or idle but as a way of building up a strong personality and of rising into those spheres which distinguish man from animal. The great festivals in life as well as the daily festive moments should be filled with a spiritual attitude which should concentrate on deepening the sense of mutuality and the appreciation of the personal identity of each individual. For this reason, and not out of any contempt for worldly goods and pleasures, I considered a simple style of living one of the most important sources of human happiness. A person who spends too much time and energy on arranging the details of the material things of life, of his house, clothes, food and other needs, has neither time nor energy to participate creatively in this great community idea and in the festive spirit which should be the goal and supreme aspiration of every culture. Although I had not previously considered that these ideas had any general validity, they had nevertheless always been my own guideline: as little as possible for personal everyday living which should, however, be organised in a completely modern way, and as much as possible for the daily building up of the communal culture which should culminate in festivities and celebrations and be intimately bound up with the development of the self. I had no doubt that the performing artist in particular, and even more so the dancer, could only fulfil his task in a deeper sense if he considered all his ways and actions to be preparation and part of festive culture.[37]

*Readers interested in the place of festivals and their psychological importance would find Alan McGlashen's defence of carnival in *The Savage and Beautiful County* of interest. McGlashen writes 'Perhaps, after all, Carnival, the answer given by so many earlier civilizations, is the best we can do. For all its look of lunacy and its inherent dangers, it is an answer that rises up from the deepest levels of the psyche. The phantoms of carnival are direct unmeditated creations of the dreaming mind.'

The examples I gave earlier may seem far removed from urban life, television-culture and our large examination-obsessed Comprehensive schools, yet in the nature of things children in any school have to move, at critical junctures, from one level to another. Perhaps teachers should develop ways not only of making these changes clear but also of making them the opportunities for symbolizing, and thereby conferring a richness and depth to the shared rhythms of ordinary life? We need to develop, particularly in our drab secondary schools, a sense of ceremonial occasion. Perhaps, to make the suggestion a little more concrete, we need to introduce into each term a major festival exploring a major theme in which children and teachers collaboratively work on a programme of events. Such festivals might well tap and draw upon the deep, symbolic needs of the human mind and provide the occasions for the community to experience its own power, its potential identity. Ceremonies could be developed in relationship to the natural cycle of Winter, Spring, Summer and Autumn, in relationship also to historical, local and religious events and occasions.

But such ceremonies, while necessary for the life of the community, are not sufficient: they need, as I have argued, complementing by another mode of symbolizing, which is in the first place personal and experiential, and which I have described more fully elsewhere.* Here the formidable aim of the teacher of the living arts is to promote among his pupils a fidelity to their own experience, whether actual or imaginative, and to all that slumbers within it. The very word 'experience' suggests in its etymological roots (*ex-periri*: to try out) the nature of this concern. The aim of the arts, seen not in the first instance as the detached study of symbolic forms but as the active effort to create and express the actual meanings and feelings which exist among the children, is to encourage the 'trying out' of symbols; the trying out of words or colours or shapes or movements or sounds. This 'trying out' can be described as 'initiation' in the Hirstian sense, except that it is an initiation not into cognitive object-centred symbolism but into expressive symbolism. The criteria here is not how does this concept relate to the intrinsic forms of the objective discipline I am studying, but rather, how does this form relate to my actual experience, my own subjectivity?

*See *English Teaching: An Expressive Discipline* in *English in Education*, Volume II, Number 3. Also Chapter 3 of *Root and Blossom*.

The expressive disciplines, in other words, are not there to secure an understanding of a pre-existing order. They are not primarily concerned with the reproduction of what is; they are concerned to inaugurate, to usher in the new and the unique. The most obvious characteristic of the arts is that they are stubbornly specific, not convertible into generalities, are imbued with all the qualities of their creators. 'The style is the man', said Flaubert, and we should add '*this* man and no other'. Art is the elaboration of the self through symbolic form. This elaboration is no easy matter: it requires a discipline and methods as exacting, however different, as any demanded by the more objective studies. Above all, it requires a certain open paucity of mind, a willingness to suspend judgement, a readiness to live with fragments and submerged half-thoughts, a commitment to living with work-in-process. And this creative receptivity – 'negative capability', as Keats called it – requires a context of trust, in which 'mistakes' can be made, explored and used for the true development of the self. For, in the end, art acts as a metaphor as well as a preparation for the greatest art of all, *the art of giving form to existence*. And this, ultimately, is why the expressive disciplines should lie at the heart of any curriculum.

On Mass-Culture, Mimesis and the Education of Feeling

Children have an inborn capacity for sympathy. But that sympathy has to be cultivated . . . And it is this point that the mass-media trample on. Even before the natural feelings of compassion have a chance to develop, the fascination of overpowering and hurting others is displayed in endless profusion. Before the soil is prepared for sympathy, the seeds of sadism are planted.

FREDERIC WERTHAM

On the whole there has been a coherence in the main stream of human mimesis; we have imitated the things we admired, and our admirations have developed further on more or less similar lines. We have formed ideals, and our ideals have guided us. It is this power of idealism, this curious power of seeing what we like or admire and then trying to imitate it; seeing things that were beautiful and trying to make others like them; seeing things that roused interest or curiosity and trying by the mimetic imagination to get inside them and understand them; that has been the great guiding force in the upward movement of humanity. The direction we take depends on the things we choose to imitate; and the choice depends on the sort of persons we really are: and what we are, again, depends on what we choose to imitate. By mimesis we make both ourselves and the world. The whole art of behaviour, or conduct itself, is a poesis which is also a mimesis. For every act we perform is a new thing made, a new creation, which has never been seen on earth before; and yet each one is an imitation of some model and an effort after some aim.

GILBERT MURRAY

THREE

Mass-Culture and Mimesis

I

Quite recently, I asked a group of thirteen teachers, representing different disciplines and teaching in different schools, to jot down their responses to the following questions:

1. What sort of influence would you say mass-culture, taken as a whole, exerts on the child/adolescent in our society?
2. As a teacher, how do you regard this influence?
3. Do you think the school should actively concern itself with mass-culture? If so, why and in what manner? If not, why not?

I had not discussed mass-culture with them, and I was not expecting the answers that came. I was not expecting such a consistency of response, nor was I expecting to find the degree of confusion and moral concern which all expressed:

Let me quote a few characteristic excerpts:

> Mass-culture has changed our way of life . . . children are bombarded by mass-culture and it has more impact now than parents or school influence at times. . . . Adolescents are attracted by the superhuman, larger than life features of mass-culture and these can give the individual a wrong impression of life in general. Things can appear too easy to obtain . . . [mass-culture] answers all problems too simply and can expose individuals to situations they are not ready to face up to, emotionally, socially and psychologically.
>
> (TEACHER A)

> Sometimes the adverts on ITV seem as popular with the children as the actual programmes and even quite young children know the jingles just as the older generation knew nursery rhymes when young. They often bring them into their games in the playground. In particular the children seem to notice adverts aimed at them – the latest flavour of crisps, chocolate bars, etc. . . . and I have no doubt helps to determine how they spend their pocket money. With the older children pop music and the latest fashions are of interest.
>
> (TEACHER B)

It seems to me that the influence of mass-culture is far reaching in its effects upon young people. There is a potency about it which has an immediacy of appeal. It is easily assimilated, it serves to create solidarity of feeling among teenagers, in particular, it would appear to cross class boundaries and be part of the fabric of peer group conformity. The worlds of television (and commercial television in particular), pop music, mass-produced clothing, advertising, magazines, football support are both a comforting means of identifying with other people in a readily acceptable exchange of shared interests and an easy kind of adrenalin. The things I mention are the currency of conversation among young people. They produce a value system which is hard for a teenager to resist.

(TEACHER C)

A tremendous terrifying influence that far too often distorts the truth, glamourises life and, most important of all, indoctrinates . . . Our modern society is infinitely better informed generally than previous societies so there must be a good influence. All communication is improved and international understanding is better . . . The popular themes of today's culture for the masses are topics such as sport, violence and sex. Obviously too much exposure to TV, books, films, etc., must lead the adolescent to puzzled confusion about the values of life beyond these, to them, desirable elements. Discretion on the part of the suppliers is vital but can we rely on this discretion when finance is all-important?

(TEACHER D)

In writing, the stereotyped values and heroes crop up repeatedly and the television jargon appears in vocabulary. . . . In arts subjects . . . children draw what they see or feel or want to be and this is influenced by what they see on television or read in comics or magazines. . . . I don't want to actively concern school work with mass-culture, but I have to recognise it's there. I don't like it because in art subjects it seems to stifle original and creative thinking.

(TEACHER E)

As a junior school teacher I ran discos two lunch times per week and escaped home to mid-day concert on the other three. . . . Schools should withstand what is shoddy and second-rate but using what the child knows we perhaps find ways to reach that child.

(TEACHER F)

Such unrehearsed comments speak for themselves. They reveal cultures in conflict. They reveal confusion. They reveal the teachers' awareness of the formidable pressures now exerted by the mass-media on the child's consciousness. I think these teachers, and the many other teachers they represent, are basically right, and in this essay I intend to place their immediate responses to my questions in a wider context. I want to sketch a theory about cultural imitation and to place that theory in the context of our own culture. In doing this I am merely extending and relating the perceptive comments I have just quoted, and at the same time attempting to ground the argument in a more comprehensive theory. I will begin by considering the nature of mass-culture.

II

The dominant culture of our times is mass-culture – a culture manufactured in cities and distributed through the mass-communications (through television, through newspapers, through cinema and radio) across the country. Mass-culture is often named 'popular culture' but this description is deceptive, for it conceals the fact that, unlike traditional folk-culture (which it often seeks to simulate) mass-culture is not made by the populace, nor does it generally express the authentic experience of a particular people. Where, we can ask, are the 'pop' artefacts which actually reflect, celebrate, order, question and relate the diverse experiences of a people? Where are the pop art-forms which incarnate the experience of people at work, of people in relationship, of people living in quite specific landscapes or townscapes during equally specific phases of time? How many 'pop' songs can we find about birth, marriage, about death? Almost none. The content of most pop songs would seem to be, significantly, confined to adolescent dream-sexuality, and here too the songs are invariably vague, stereotyped and, in truth, more infantile than adolescent ('baby, baby, baby'). In *The Primitive and The Civilized* (Tract 18) Stanley Diamond claimed that in pop music we find 'love as an abstraction rather than the actual loving of a person as a being in the world'. And it is the same unreal love, sentimental, evasive, stereotyped, that we find manufactured week after week in the teenage magazines which litter the shelves of our newsagents. In true culture we invariably find a high degree of specificity, a strong sense of context, of time and location, a sense of unique relationships, of binding existential meanings; in false culture we tend to find the reverse, we find a high degree of generality in which all things prickly, problematic and diverse have been conveniently dissolved.

What we need to know is how mass-culture influences the

young; how, for example, it affects the way in which they come to perceive, interpret and create their world. It is often asserted that mass-culture has little substantial influence on the child/adolescent/adult. My argument moves in the opposite direction. I will attempt to show that mass-culture, like any other culture, not only influences the young but actually provides the frame within which they sketch their lives, and is intended to do so. In this context I will look, in some detail, at the influence of advertising, and consider the dangers of the young being exposed to publications and productions which preach the pleasures of pure violence, of the clenched fist, the boot and the knife.

I want, however, to begin and end the argument by considering what is and what ought to be the relationship between mass-culture and education. What should be the function of the school during a period of cultural debasement? That is the question we must seek to answer. At the moment, as I now wish to show, many people are, consciously or unconsciously, evading that question and the momentous challenge it constitutes.

III

I believe that in our schools we still put too much emphasis on knowledge and too little on culture. In our schools – and particularly in our secondary schools – what matters is the ability to master the formal content of particular subjects, not the ability to refine, relate and discipline the intuitive, emotional, sensuous and pre-conceptual responses of the growing child. Of course, it is true that some time may be allocated to cultural activities, but these are generally either extra-curricular or seen as 'soft-options'. And there can be little doubt that as education moves away from the nursery school it becomes steadily more abstract, shedding as it goes emotional and sensuous qualities. Our schools are essentially preoccupied with knowledge and know-how – with facts, figures, modes of classification and methods of examination. At the present moment, a utilitarian Government and a philosophically blind and culturally ignorant group of *Black Paper* writers (the Left and Right, as usual, mirroring each other most faithfully) by suggesting that our schools have become too free and too expression-centred are creating a most misleading image of our educational institutions.

The truth is that our secondary schools are still remarkably functional and exam-orientated. I have indicated in the opening essays how the expressive disciplines – disciplines concerned primarily with the refinement of subjectivity – lie on the very edges of the school curriculum, insecure, unsupported and often unsure of their proper purposes.

As a result of the demand for cognitive study, for the neutral, unimaginative accumulation of fragments of knowledge, the adolescent is obliged to go elsewhere for his personal culture. And, as we know, he doesn't have very far to go or, indeed, have much choice in the matter. In the newsagents, the highly popular magazines for adolescent girls, which bind cosmetics, fashion, pop-music and romance into one dreamy gestalt proliferate. At the local cinema one can see the endless sequences of sensational 'X' films they view. Add to the magazines and films, BBC1, ITV and BBC2 television, the recordings of 'pop hits' on disc and cassette, and, behind these, the all-pervasive influences of advertising and publicity, and we have a crude map of the commercial culture to which the great majority of adolescents are deeply and uncritically attached.

If, under the influence of the school, the adolescent's rational knowledge about the world is being slowly extended, we must realize at the same time that his emotional attitudes to life are being shaped by another pressure, a force alien to the sober routine of school, and possessing greater energy in that it appeals, however crudely, to the irrational level of the human mind. I am suggesting that there is a rift in our society between knowledge and passion, between fact and ritual, which we must become aware of and come to terms with. Given this rift, it is not altogether surprising that the adolescent, even the intelligent adolescent, sees learning as a dull, if necessary, activity and commercial culture as colourful, ritualistic, releasing; not surprising that after the day's routine at school he returns home to play the latest music full-blast; not altogether surprising that he assumes that it is the glossy products of mass-culture and not the studies at school which embody the quintessential rhythms and inner purposes of life itself.

We need to consider this division between intelligence and passion more closely. The division is clearly unhealthy. It is a symptom of disintegration. The division undermines the foundations of knowledge and true culture alike, and throws them into false opposition. If passion is sucked out of knowledge, knowledge becomes a dry and desiccated thing. At best, it becomes merely functional. And if the intellect is dismissed from the events of cultural creation and appreciation, culture can quickly deteriorate into primitive cults, into an empty cackling and crowing in the dark (witness the state of many of the contemporary arts, witness also the interest in black magic which disfigures the so-called 'counter-culture'). Culture, if it is to reach out and mature through a creative process which continually endeavours to integrate diverse expressive possibilities into unified wholes, depends on the habit of intelligent criticism, the help of sympathetic but penetrating discourse. At crucial stages, the life of culture requires the critical energy of the alert mind. At the present moment, a divorce between knowledge and culture is taking place. There is a danger that the powers of the mass media and the powers of the educational system, working in isolation from each other and appealing to completely different levels of the psyche, will together conspire to create a man who is at once technically knowledgeable and culturally infantile. Functional civilization may squat heavily in the centre of such a man's brain, but Caliban-like impulses, inchoate and dangerously confused, will beat through his undeveloped heart. The emergence of such a man, outwardly knowledgeable, inwardly blind; preoccupied with techniques and not with teleologies; responsive to the dictates of scientific progress, but not to the imperatives of human culture, should serve to unsettle us all. As I hope to show later, there is good reason to believe that even now, although we are living in a highly technical organized, highly 'educated' society (school for all, from five to sixteen), the life of our fantasies, emotions and relationships is becoming predominantly coarse, brutish and sensational, or, if not sensational, then sentimental, banal and generally vacuous. For both ends of this spectrum, the vicious and the sentimental, point to a similar corruption of authentic feeling, a similar debasement of inward experience.

I am implying, then, that the violence and crudity so frequently described and reported relates to a failure to fuse mind and passion, and that this in turn relates to a division between school and culture and, beyond that, to a failure in the cultural processes engendered by the consumer society. The latter can be pinpointed quite simply: there are large and accruing profits to be made from a vast populace rendered intellectually gullible and emotionally indolent. Cliché, sentiment, glossy patter, stereotyped images, instant jingles round the clock, are easy to manufacture, easy to slot into each other, and (providing that within the populace there are no sensitive feelings for aesthetic shape and personal truth) easy to distribute not only across 'the provinces', but around the world. There is nothing, for example, easier than to slot dead clichés together making them sound warm and intimate to lazy, half-illiterate readers: 'Every day in the super *Sun*: your best telly programme guide . . . and the star-studded stories about your top telly shows' . . . And headlines like 'Super-star Extraordinary'* for those who prefer *The Observer*.

My contention is that a sensational and vacuous culture will inevitably create a sensational and vacuous society – for culture condenses various modes of behaviour and perception and makes them not only acceptable but infinitely desirable. There is a direct relationship between the state of consciousness of the individual and the cultural forms which he has internalized from his society. Our universe is structured through symbols, and, necessarily, our symbols are taken from the society into which we are born. If, say, a person only hears clichés during the formative period of his development, he will inevitably speak in clichés, and while he speaks in clichés, his mind will never be able to penetrate beyond the trite and commonplace. It is impossible to think politically in the two-syllable or ejaculative 'wow-pow' language of popular journalism. When we see in the *Sun* politics presented as pantomime, as Dracula 'X' films, as spectacle and entertainment, surrounded by advertising copy 'What the guys are buying for their girls', by French models, complete with such slogans as 'Forward with the people', we must point out that such a manner of symbolizing political information ensures the death of politics as a complex matter of understanding and evaluation. 'Forward with the people' in this context can only mean 'Forward with mobocracy' and, in invisible ink, 'For it profits Rupert Murdoch'. Such papers – and the success of the *Sun* has brought all daily papers, desperate for circulation, that much nearer the gutter

*What a debasement of language is revealed in *The Observer*'s headline! First we have the word 'star' to denote brilliance, a good, if overworked, metaphor, then, as that word becomes over-used and abused, we have 'super-star', then 'Super-star Extraordinary'. In this manner words become more and more redundant and we pile up phrase upon phrase to say less and less.

– seek to titillate and entertain, and insidiously control by all that they exclude.

What I am anxious to demonstrate is that the symbol educates. The symbol opens up certain ways of seeing the world and closes other ways. It influences our behaviour by first of all cutting out those channels down which our thoughts, feelings and expectations flow. Depending on the energy a symbol harbours, it can contract or expand, deepen or make shallow, our human universe. This is a crucial observation. It provides the critic with an essential key: with it we are able to penetrate beyond the seemingly harmless exterior of commercial culture. If we take language as our example of symbolism, it is not difficult to appreciate that any one language tends to incarnate a very particular way of being-in-the-world. The Greek language expressed and continually reinforced a rational disposition of mind, so that it is not surprising that Greek civilization culminated in the great abstract achievements of metaphysics, mathematics and law. The very word used by the Greeks to denote the universe, *cosmos*, also denoted order and beauty. How, then, could the Greeks, using this word, feel that the world might be chaotic, unpredictable and absurd? The Greeks assumed that life was as ordered and lucid as the complex symmetrical patterns of their own language. Thus, as Professor Kitto has pointed out, they always sought to generalize the issue. In contrast, if Ezra Pound is right, the Chinese language with its visual and concrete character tended to keep experience close to the sensuous, the immediate, the palpable. It is also quite conceivable that the Chinese language, not possessing the sharp split, as in Western languages, between subject - verb - object, I - doing something to - IT, did not foster that painful sense of cleavage between self and world which has been one of the traumatic experiences of Western Man.

Again, it is possible to examine primary orientations to space and time as embodied in different languages. The English language is most discriminating with regard to time; we are not only able to place events in a sensitive past/present/future continuum, we also actually identify, with our word will, powers of intention with future reality. According to the anthropologist Edward Carpenter, the language of the Eskimo is utterly different in orientation:

> The so-called case system in Eskimo, which is as important in that language as, say, tense is in English, is concerned with position, especially

spacial relationships. The attention we lavish on time, the Eskimo accords to space.[38]

The central principle illustrated by these fleeting examples has been expressed by the linguist Edward Sapir and by the philosopher Ernst Cassirer. Sapir wrote, 'Language is heuristic, its forms predetermine for us certain modes of observation and interpretation.'[39] Cassirer claimed, 'Our perceptions, intuitions, and concepts have coalesced with the terms and speech forms of our mother tongue.'[40]

Even more generally, we could say that individual experience is not given but is made, that it is made through the active and personal use of symbols but that these symbols, are, for the most part, inherited and carry with them a hidden cargo of attitudes, orientations, interpretations and expectations. I want later to return to the fundamental questions as to whether the symbolic forms of industrial and commercial society are adequate to life, as to whether they confine too tightly the range of consciousness and plant seeds of destruction within it. But first it is necessary to consider the way in which culture is inherited, to consider the way in which the young absorb the cultural forms which surround them and, by so doing, become members of their society. I want now, briefly, to sketch a theory about the nature of cultural transmission.

IV

Aristotle claimed that man was 'the most imitative creature in the world and learns by imitation'. In conduct he saw the same formative principle at work: 'each seeks to transfer to himself the traits he admires in the other'. We have only to watch a two-year-old child enthusiastically reproducing nearly all the actions of his parents, brothers or sisters to realize the truth of Aristotle's remarks. Often a child will imitate an action he has just seen without having any sense of its purpose, and his ability to do so gives him a sense of joyful delight. The child will chuckle with satisfaction at his achievement. It is his way of entering the social world which encompasses him. Looking at a child as a cultural being, we could say that a child imitates before he comprehends, and through imitation eventually comes to comprehend. The child imitates sounds before he understands meanings. A year or even years before he can read, a child will pick up a blank sheet of paper, look down and, as it were, 'read', confidently throwing out a babble of sound. The child is imitating, and thus anticipating what will eventually become the actual pleasure of reading a letter. First imitation, then realization. It has been commonly observed that when children play with dolls they transfer to them the values and characteristic preoccupations of their parents; in this way children explore the future tasks they will be expected to tackle. Their play with dolls is a rehearsal for the play of life. The imitation is not purely mechanical, never wholly predictable – for there is often an element of improvisation in the child's act. This is why I prefer to describe the process in which the child reproduces for himself what he sees in his immediate cultural environment as the process of mimesis.

The concept mimesis suggests the presence of dramatic and expressive qualities; it is related, of course, to the verbs 'to mime' and 'to mimic'. To be able to mimic one must not only be able successfully to reproduce the characteristic gestures of a particular person but also at the same time to ridicule them – i.e., offer a creative interpretation of what has been accurately observed. I point this out to emphasize *the creativity latent within the mimetic process*. The creativity may be developed or suppressed, used or abused – but it is always there, a hidden energy which great teachers have always appealed to. It is important to stress here this hidden energy because it is vital to realize that while culture makes man, man also makes and remakes culture. In this essay I am stressing the social powers of culture, the powers particularly of commercial culture to invade and dominate man's consciousness, but it is important not to forget the very real powers of the individual to transform himself within his own culture.* However, what he cannot do is transform himself outside culture. What also seems certain is that as a common culture becomes exhausted so it becomes progressively more difficult for the individual to keep himself alert and whole. There is, in brief, a continuous and necessary interplay between the life of the

*I will return to these powers to transcend in the third section of this book, where I will attempt to sketch an existential view of education. One compelling example of creative mimesis is provided by Edmund Gosse in his autobiography *Father and Son*.

general culture and the life of the individual; to impoverish one is to impoverish the other. In his brilliant essay 'Culture Genuine and Spurious' Edward Sapir expressed this relationship as follows:

> There is no sound and vigorous individual incorporation of a cultural ideal without the soil of a genuine communal culture: and no genuine communal culture without the transforming energies of personalities at once robust and saturated with the cultural values of their time and place.[41]

It would seem that through a prolonged process of mimesis the child internalizes all the main forms of his culture. Through mimesis the child, born defenceless and with few instincts beyond the instinct to suck, becomes a full member of his particular society. When, for instance, in a primitive tribe the child listens, with all the other members of society, to the storyteller, all the beliefs and customs of his tribe are being dramatically and poetically conveyed to him. The stories, the proverbs, the songs, the chants, even the rhythm and syntax and vocabulary of the language in which they are couched, celebrate and define a most particular way of being-in-the-world, as do the carvings, the masks, the music, the dances, the rituals. By spontaneously assimilating and reproducing the dominant forms of his culture, the child unconsciously assimilates at the same time the particular unified vision of his community.

In ancient Greece, we know that the whole population – men, women, adolescents, children, babies – attended the great tragedies. The theatres were built to accommodate the whole city, not just one social class. The plays were not truffles for the few, but substantial food to be inwardly digested by a whole people. And we know that after the plays were shown in the city they then toured the provinces, so that no-one might be left untouched and untaught by the art of the age. From Plato's critical commentary we also discover that the Greeks knew their Homer by heart, and referred to his works 'for all the conduct and culture of human life'. Children growing up in Greece had no choice but to speak in a language enriched and purified by the great poets and dramatists, no choice but to have their eyes educated by the indigenous architecture, the surrounding statues, the all-encompassing patterns of a unified culture. There was no question of choice – the child was immersed in the cultural high-tide of his age.

Each community provides its own examples of a mimetic process. In nineteenth-century England a knowledge of classical culture was still an essential part of learning, at least for the upper classes in the public schools. Children were surrounded by classical texts, and learnt them by heart. Classical myth, poetry and philosophy provided the essential references and imagery through which the young, as they matured, could interpret their own experience and their own age. As George Steiner has put it, 'The meaning of present context with classic text, served as an indispensible mechanism of self-consciousness.' A headmaster of Winchester in the nineteenth century put the belief like this: 'Classical learning is the inheritance of all former ages. Combined with its allied subjects of philology and history, it puts a person into the possession of all the inherited wisdom of the ages.' Children brought up in nonconformist Wales were given the Bible as their map of being, and it was to this sacred text, as disseminated through the tiny Welsh-speaking chapels, that they were expected to refer for moral bearings and inspiration. In both cases, English public schools and Welsh chapel, so different in so many ways, a certain psychological orientation which might be summarized as a reverent looking back to the written word – a deep respect for inherited text and the meaning of the word – was quite unconsciously transmitted, and marked the age.*

In writing about the importance and manner of mimesis I am, of course, expressing nothing new. Shelley in his *Defense of Poetry* wrote about the need for 'edifying patterns for general imitation' and, reflecting on the Greeks, declared:

> Homer embodied the ideal perfection of his age in human character; nor can we doubt that those who read his verses were awakened to an ambition of becoming like to Achilles, Hector, and Ulysses; the truth and beauty of friendship, patriotism, and persevering devotion to an object, were unveiled to the depths in these immortal creations: *the sentiments of the auditors must have been refined and enlarged by a sympathy with such great and lovely impersonations, until from admiring they imitated, and from imitation they identified themselves with the objects of their admiration.*[42] (My italics)

*I do not want to be misunderstood here. I am in no way suggesting that we can or should return to these conditions. The nonconformism of Wales was intolerably narrow: the public schools were intolerably competitive and brutish. However, both provide clear patterns of mimesis. Also I suspect the tendency to look back into time at cultural achievements for understanding possessed a shrewdness and wisdom which we have largely lost. But, more generally, there can be no simple return to past conditions. The way forward must always be through the present conditions and must represent a *transformation* rather than reproduction of what has gone before.

Nietzsche called for the poet who would 'divine those cases where . . . a great noble soul is still possible . . . where it may become permanent, visible and representative of a type and so by the stimulus to imitation and envy help to create the future.'[43]

Goethe maintained, 'Everything great moulds us from the moment we become aware of it.'[44]

If we allow the rough corollary to Goethe's assertion, everything base debases us as soon as we respond to it, then we find ourselves facing once again our informing principle, culture educates.*

We are now in a position to consider in more detail the nature and power of contemporary mass-culture. Here it is certainly not difficult to find simple and convincing examples of mimesis. The following is part of a description of a David Bowie 'concert':

> He [Bowie] has abandoned his Ziggy Stardust style and now dresses simply in baggy black trousers, vest and white shirt – a transformation which has taken some of his fans by surprise because *hundreds turned up at Wembley last week wearing make-up, lurex and other manifestations of a past Bowie* . . . The audience obviously is predominantly teenage . . . with the younger teenagers tending to be working class and the older ones students.[45] (My italics)

One could list many examples showing how various styles are made – through publicity working on market forces – fashionable, and then widely emulated.** It is even possible to document examples of individuals acting out, in the most faithful mimicry, events, including rape and murder, witnessed on television and film. It is, however, essential that our general understanding of mimesis is not reduced to a simple cause and

*Goethe's own work, in fact, provides us with a disturbing example of mimesis. A number of individuals committed suicide following the heroic example set in his book *The Sorrows of Young Werther*.

**Elvis Presley provides one dramatic example. His gyrations and gestures disseminated through the new electronic media – in the hands of commercialism – became the crude symbolic forms of identification for a whole generation. It will be remembered how thousands of adolescents cut their hair in the pattern of the duck-tail in complete imitation of their master. The mimetic process is perpetually used in a commerical society where culture has become a saleable commodity. Under the pressure of the conveyor-belt cultural forms are in a constant state of change, they become ephemeral items and can possess no enduring power or purpose beyond profits and more profits. At the moment of writing Punk has entered into the conveyor-belt process. Tomorrow it will be another brand-name, and then another.

effect analysis, of artefact *x* causing action *y*. What we must rather insist on is the general tendency of man to be deeply influenced by that which culturally surrounds him.

Thus, with the concept of mimesis at the back of our minds, we need to ask broad questions directed at the totality of our cultural environment. We need to consider commercial culture as a whole. We need to discover how a child's sensibility is affected when he grows up in a family where Radio 1 blares out most of the day and TV images flicker most of the night. We need to ask what parts of the child's mind and body are being alerted and trained by his cultural environment. What parts are being numbed? What parts remain untouched, and thereby atrophy? We need to enquire how the child's mind is affected by the poetry and mythology of advertising. We need to know whether television, by providing so much detail and that so constantly, effaces imagination and, in so doing, develops a deep passivity of mind, an unwillingness to grapple with life, an inability to initiate events. We need to know whether the casual stance adopted by the intelligent young today derives from a profound sense of cultural relativity fostered by the arbitrary flow of the serious and the trivial, the real and the unreal, which marks television entertainment, magazines, newspapers and radio alike. Today's university students form the first TV generation, and they would seem to manifest a fear of deep seriousness and deep feeling. Is there a connection between the casual stance of the student and television? We need to know whether the electronic medium with its instantaneity and completeness precludes the development of inward space. We know that the reading of literature demands privacy, and calls upon complex powers of imaginative reconstruction, and thereby tends to develop a sense of inwardness. Is it true that what comes through electronic culture does not demand or foster the same qualities? Is it possible also that in thousands of homes television has now become the dominant socializing force, having more influence even than the surrounding family?

What is certain is that if the nineteenth century was essentially a verbal culture, referring back to the past, the twentieth century is essentially a visual and sound culture pointing ever forwards. Television has been responsible for vast changes in human sensibility. It is not a neutral force. It is probably impossible at this point in history to understand all the complex changes and their many ramifications. I want, however, to limit my attention to two important elements in the present transmission of cultural forms to the young. The first concerns the influence of advertising, the second the influence of violence.

V

The Canadian critic Northrop Frye has warned us:

> It is quite possible . . . for communications media, especially the newer electronic ones, to break down the associative structures of the inner mind and replace them with the prefabricated structures of the media.[46]

This, quite simply, is one of the main intentions of the advertising companies. They are concerned to impress on the child's mind patterns and word clusters long before he goes to school, even before he has mastered his own language. Officials for advertising express the intentions of the copywriters like this:

> With television we began to sell our product before they (the children) could talk. They know who the TV characters are before they can say full sentences.
>
> Children love their heroes, and if a hero says, 'Eat Wheaties', they will – for years and years and years. To be able to capitalize on a fad, a company has to be able to move in and out fast.
>
> If you want to create your own hard-hitting spokesman to children, the most effective is the super-hero-miracle-worker. . . . A child must be able to mimic his hero, whether he is James Bond, Superman or Dick Tracy: to be able to fight and shoot without punishment or guilt feelings.[47]

The insistence that the child 'must be able to mimic his hero' asserts in a thoroughly commercial context my main argument, that a child learns about his society and himself through a process of mimesis. Commercial agents are consciously taking over the traditional function of poets and priests in order to fabricate a secular mythology for the production and consumption of goods. The success of the counterfeit mythology depends on the degree to which the copywriters can encourage the child to internalize and reproduce his 'super-heroes'. There are reasons to believe that advertising helps to shape the child's evolving consciousness.

Recent research in America has shown that the majority of children sing not nursery rhymes but television commercials. Furthermore, it was revealed that, by the age of three, nine out of ten children can identify all the main advertising television cartoon-characters. In Britain, where the bombardment of advertising is still considerably less than in America, commercial art is having a similar effect. A student in a Welsh-speaking school (and that context is important) was alarmed when, on the mention of a particular cereal, the whole class burst out singing the English jingle used in the TV advertisement. Stimuli-response! I have heard of drama classes where children left to their own resources will faithfully insert advertisements between the acts of their own play. The Advisory Centre for Education, examining hundreds of letters written by small children to Father Christmas some years ago, declared it was disturbed 'by the number of six-year-old girls who wanted "sexy boots" and "pop records"', and concluded 'that a teenage concern with body odour seems to have been successfully planted on little girls by mass advertising'.

An obsession with fashion and cosmetics would seem to inform many adolescent fantasies of sexual relationships. The images in *Jackie* and *Petticoat* educate the eye to look for certain characteristics in the loved one. The idyllic settings of romantic love foster dreams and expectations which the text interpets according to the religion of consumption. The following passage, written by a fourteen-year-old girl in response to the title 'My Ideal Boyfriend', indicates the power such advertising can have on the adolescent mind.

> . . . I don't mind little moustaches, to be dressed in smart brown flares with turn-ups, single breasted jackets. He must wear Benshires mens and above all, if he doesn't wear Brut I don't go for him.

The imperatives are not emotional, moral or religious, not personal in any way. What the adolescent looks for, what she wants, derive competely from the advertising industry. The girl has internalized the image of manhood as concocted by the copywriters, and seeks to find the man who approximates to that image in real life. One couldn't wish for a clearer or more disturbing example of mimesis.

Advertising is thus clearly having a salient influence on those growing up in our society. All manner of experiences are being stapled to consumer products. Such a process must debase experience itself – for love, by all definitions, is not a response to a perfume or to flared trousers and single-breasted jackets: to make it seem that it is destroys the meaning of the symbol, and in so doing diminishes man.

The symbolism of advertising, like that of political propaganda, seeks to gain a hold over the underdeveloped mind by suggestion, simplification, stereotype, repetition and deception. It is a symbolism which is utterly inadequate to the needs of existence. In promising what it cannot give, advertising erodes trust and the language of trust and promotes a style of life as voracious as it is empty. Defending the Osmonds, a young fan writes to *Radio Times*:

> I've got Donny's, Alan's, Merrill's and Jay's autographs along with 47 badges, one Donny hat, one mug, all their singles and LP's, pillow-cases, Donny pennant, two Donny scarves, T-shirts, one Osmond jacket, trousers, shoes, Donny ring, pendant, rosettes, money-box, lampshade, belt, writing paper. . . . They do everything they can to prove their love for us.[48]

Through the process of mimesis, powerfully manipulated by commercial élites, the young are growing up with a prefabricated culture which is making them stupid.

What I am describing here, the successful reproduction of the dominant cultural forms by the young, seems, on my own terms, all but inevitable. Advertising is the symbolic and ritualistic form of the consumer economy. What choice, then, have most children, educated as they are by their surrounding cultural environment? What choice is there in cultural matters? Survey after survey shows us what we already know; that the young dislike school; that they do not read much (over a quarter of sixteen-year-olds never read a book outside school); that they watch television voraciously (the most time-consuming leisure activity of sixteen-years-olds is watching television, which two-thirds of them do 'often'); that their most popular programme is *Top of the Pops*; that they enjoy spending money on clothes, cosmetics and consumer goods. We know this because we know what an industrial consumer economy demands from people. It demands that we buy life over the counter. It demands passivity. It demands conformity. It demands a widespread, self-satisfied stupidity.

The American sociologist Jules Henry, examining his own society, put it like this:

> Homo sapiens trains his children for the roles they will fill as adults. This is as true of the Eskimo three-year-old who is encouraged to stick his little spear into a dead polar bear as it is of an American child of the same age who turns on TV to absorb commercials, the one will be a skilled hunter, the other a virtuoso consumer.[49]

But a virtuoso consumer is not a human being, he is an automaton. Nor can any future society survive if it insists on the unrestrained and mindless habits of mass-production and mass-consumption. The symbols of industrial culture have become the symbols of annihilation, of individual and world annihilation. But the young must imitate them because other symbols, pointing elsewhere, have all but disappeared or, if they have not disappeared, seem to stand at the very edges of 'normal life', strange and inaccessible.

VI

Alongside the continuous chaining of personal qualities to consumer trivia, a growing emphasis on violence is to be discerned in contemporary culture. In films, in paperbacks, in imported American comics, in certain pop-performances, violence, sometimes ritualistic in form, sometimes realistic, is constantly portrayed. An issue of the magazine *Honey* describing itself as 'the magazine for young people: the emphasis is on service to the reader' (read each month by 25,000 fifteen-year-olds) recently entertained its audience by describing the antics of the pop-star Alice Cooper.

> In the finale of his stage act Alice embraces his black-clad executioner before being beheaded, and other members of the group eat his body while the executioner wipes the blood off his hands.[50]

In other performances, Alice Cooper filled plastic dolls with blood and then, at the end of his 'show', cut off their heads with a large sword. The David Bowie 'concert' to which I have already referred began, we are told:

> with a thirties-style cartoon film tastefully depicting an eye in close-up – being sliced by a razor. At 8.30 Bowie's . . . musicians appear, punching out what seemed to be a million decibels of noise.[51]

'Permissive' society permits such spectacles, and the commercial powers, excited by each new excess, each new release of shocking experience, relay it across the country. It is pertinent to notice how the *Daily Express, Daily Mirror* ('Mirror Pop Exclusive – Sex and Bowie') and BBC television, for nearly a whole hour, rushed to give publicity to Bowie's cultural feast. Here indeed we find that advertising, publicity, sensationalism and news have become all but one. The methods of advertising have become the methods of journalism. And journalism itself often becomes little more than a smooth vehicle for promoting commercial products and commercial events. All the forms of commercial culture are bound together by a strict, if hidden, morphological relationship, a relationship predicated on the common belief in profits, investment, turnover, cash-flow, more profits, etc. In fact, advertising not only provides the capital for most forms of mass-culture in our society, it also provides, as we have seen, the unifying ritual and daily sacrament. Industrial culture possesses no imperative beyond 'more and more', and hence it is powerless to evaluate ethically its own dangerous if 'economically successful' products. In *Towards a Critique of Industrial Culture* (Tract 15) Seymor Betsky defined this, the central dilemma of industrial culture, as follows:

> What we have, in effect, is a culture without a central intelligence, without comprehending mind, without a sense of order and control. So long as each industrial culture achieves enough of a standard of living to satisfy enough people, it appears to be interested in no further dimension in its way of life.[52]

Indeed, in order to secure profits and what it misleadingly calls 'a standard of living', industrial culture is quite content to undermine all traditional morality, and to invert all values and human meanings, if by so doing it can increase the levels of production and consumption. For the one unifying imperative in industrial culture is 'Produce-Consume-Produce-Consume-Produce'. How can such a culture possibly evaluate the human effects of its own endless flow of products?

In his recent book *Fellow Teachers* Philip Rieff compares the present state of Western culture with that of late Roman culture where, he points out, the proletariat as well as the aristocracy learned to enjoy watching animals, and then humans, tortured in massive, public, state-financed arenas. He names the mass-viewing of Christians, mauled and eaten by lions as 'the ultimate staging of *Oh, Calcutta*!' The imagery provided by the books our adolescents read under the desks celebrates the same sort of sensationalism, but sinks it in the slum-gutters and between drab walls of the mass-production factories. This is the description taken from the back of the paperback *Chopper*:

> Chopper moved into position. The skinhead was still bent double. Bringing up his knee, Chopper felt with satisfaction the scrunch of broken bone as the kid's nose made contact. The kid went down, while blows from boots rained upon his body. He lay groaning, spitting out gouts of deep red blood and pieces of broken teeth.[53]

The writing follows a formula. The blunt, mostly monosyllabic words *kid, boots, scrunch, gout, Chopper*, are there to provoke a coarse excitement. The companion volume to *Chopper, Skinhead*, was reprinted seven times within three months of its first publication!

In a society where impoverished cultural forms – and those mostly corrupt and dishonest – are conveyed to the young, the attraction of violence must be obvious; it portrays a quick solution to the anxiety of not being able to communicate. The need to symbolize is thus bypassed – but it is a short cut which eliminates the vital foundations of all community life. There must often come a point in our society when the adolescent, moved by some sudden leap of feeling or some thought stirring in the obscure darkness of his own mind, cannot find the words he needs, and so is incapable of grasping that feeling or that thought and of revealing it – and thus his deepest self – to other people. This inability makes him feel a stranger to himself. It frustrates him, locks him in, humiliates him. Violence offers a release from such existential loneliness. Finding civilized and elaborate forms of communication impossible, the adolescent resorts to crude and desperate methods to demonstrate his existence and to mask his impotence. As he is unable to assert himself through the means of culture, which have never been properly developed, he comes to assert himself through the primitive thrust of the body, the boot and the fist. Such a strategy, legitimized by mass-culture, where the victors are invariably characterized by their toughness and their readiness to kill 'without guilt feelings', heralds the end of culture and morality.

Recent reports suggest that the amount of violence in schools is increasing. Teachers often observe how children moving about between lessons do not talk but assault each other, nudging, kicking, poking rulers, hurling satchels. Such activity, even if boredom be the cause, would seem to point to an inability to symbolize experience. Contact, such as it is, is physical, sensational and aggressive. A thirteen-year-old girl writes about herself, 'Each night we go out and if we see a fight or any Hell's Angels, we join in and lay the boot in which are hobnails or laceup shoes.' In the estate where the girl lived every flowering-cherry tree planted by the council had been hacked down until the council gave up the project. Because of a failure in cultural forms, the frustration obscurely and rightly sensed by the people living there had no way of finding itself. Unable to tug resentment, hatred, confusion into consciousness, into order and purpose, the disordered feelings became convoluted and hostile to the very thing most needed.

The Greeks called all those who could not master the beauty and symmetry of their own language, barbarians. The barbarians were those who before the beauty of the world and the privilege of existence could only say 'ba-ba'. Today's barbarians are those who, fed on the cheap symbolism of commercial culture, are unable to locate their true identities, and who, in resorting to strategies of violence, destroy their community from within. In some schools in America the teacher is protected by armed guards. When schools depend on the police for their authority, the educational process, grounded in trust, has come to a deplorable end. That the violence in our society is often given form and sanction by commercial culture there can be no doubt. What we must realize is that, as in all other societies, a mimetic process is taking place, a process in which harsh and thuggish values are being internalized and, in varying degrees, acted out. This process is only held in check by an older culture, by customs and values connected to religion, to the arts, properly conceived, and to the small organic communities. And, as we know, this traditional culture, these inherited forms of discourse and symbolization, are visibly and rapidly waning.

We are advancing outwardly, technologically, at the same time as we are contracting inwardly, culturally. The symptoms of decay in our society do not point so much to a failure in the distribution of incomes and possessions as to a deep and widespread failure in cultural forms.

VII

In this essay I have argued that popular culture is, for the most part, more cogently defined as mass-culture, a culture fabricated in the metropolis for commercial ends. I have tried to show that, although mass-culture is a counterfeit culture, it yet 'educates' emotions, directs fantasies, fans expectations and plants values and, in fact, does so far more effectively than our conventional schools. The process through which children tend to reproduce the dominant cultural forms I have called mimesis. In nature mimicry is a well-known method of adaptation to environment. Within a hundred years the pale peppered moth, the *Biston betularia*, changed the colour of its wings in industrial areas, to match the sooty bark of the trees on which it settled. In order to survive it became a black mutant, and did so in less than a century! An amazing example of mimicry. The hover-fly provides us with another example. The hover-fly, consumed by hungry birds, 'learnt to imitate' the yellow and black markings of the wasp (which birds find inedible) in order to preserve its own species from annihilation. These provide fascinating examples of a sort of mimetic process in nature. They present us with rich metaphors. Children, we could say, learn ways of becoming stupid in order to be considered normal in order to survive. Yet such comparisons are dangerous, for the ability to symbolize draws man out of the manifold of nature and ushers into the world the terrifying and transforming powers of consciousness. And as soon as there is individual consciousness then the laws of necessity are broken. Nature can no longer provide a key to understanding.

Another order of life is created through the ability to symbolize: an order, not necessarily against instinct, but certainly transcending it. Such qualities as authenticity, love, courage, hope, creativity, loyalty, trust, sincerity are, in large measure, cultural achievements. Here we touch upon the central principle informing this essay. And the principle is, at heart, affirmative of man, for it defines man as a maker of culture, as a creator of symbolic forms, as a mortal god. Indeed, the principle only becomes depressing when it is used to examine the state of contemporary culture. Yet even here it is not finally depressing, because to attack those conditions which imprison man is to affirm him, is, implicitly, to remind him of what he could become.

I would like, finally, to list some of the points implicit in this essay as a series of propositions. I have, in essence, been urging:

1. That individual experience is not given (as, for example, in the *tabula rasa* model of the mind) but actively created.
2. That individual experience is created through the continuous use of diverse symbols.
3. That these symbols, in the first place, are inherited and have to be absorbed and re-created by every child through a process of mimesis.
4. That these symbols carry within them a dense cargo of attitudes, beliefs, interpretations, assumptions, ways of feeling, conceiving and perceiving.
5. That in learning to imitate, use and adapt the symbolism around him, the child becomes a distinct member of his own community.

From the arguments presented in sections 4 and 5 we could, perhaps, also conclude:

6. That in traditional societies the inherited symbolism, relating to a whole way of living and dying, is powerfully transmitted, conferring unity of being but leaving little space for individual elaboration.
7. That in modern industrial society the symbolism, in the hands of the commercial élites, constantly changes styles and images but only in order to secure the voracious consumption of manufactured commodities. Hence the symbolism is corrupt and the freedom it confers illusory.

Considering these propositions in the light of the whole essay, I would like to conclude with a positive description of what would seem to be in these matters the good society. I would suggest that the good society effectively transmits a strong and authentic symbolism while allowing at the same time personal space for improvization and innovation. The good society recognizes the principle of complementarity; it seeks to secure continuity while it provokes innovation; it imparts tradition, an inherited wealth of symbolic forms, but promotes a spontaneity of being within that tradition and within those forms. The good society conceives mimesis as a twofold process, both reproductive and creative.

But from what, it will be asked, can such authentic symbolism be derived? It can, of course, only rise up from life, or rather from individual lives, seeking outside the hollow artefacts of the industrial power complex new forms of meaning, new forms of being. Yet paradoxically, and wholly in accord with my argument, these forms, should they take shape, will be re-creations and transformations of what has already been. The new forms are even now prefigured in our remote and not so remote historical past. Here again, what is required is a creative act of mimesis, a transforming of the best of the past in the light of our tormenting circumstances.

FOUR

Mass-Symbolism and Education

But there can be no stronger illusion . . . than this, that because the tools of life are today more specialized and more refined than ever before, that because the technique brought by science is more perfect than anything the world has yet known, it necessarily follows that we are in like degree attaining to a profounder harmony of life, to a deeper and more satisfying culture.

EDWARD SAPIR

The average American has learned to put in place of his inner self a high and rising standard of living, because technological drivenness can survive as a cultural configuration only if the drive towards a higher standard of living becomes internalized; only if it becomes a moral law, a kind of conscience.

JULES HENRY

I

The theme – the relationship between mass-culture and education – which I intend to explore in this essay is, of course, as vast as it is momentous. I am resigned to the fact that I will raise many issues which I will not be able to resolve, many issues which at this particular juncture, perhaps, cannot be adequately resolved. Yet it is imperative that we tackle the innumerable problems posed by mass-culture ambitiously – on a large scale; imperative that we do not scurry away to examine a tiny corner of the basement before considering the whole structure of the building. We need to envisage industrial culture as a totality, and I am afraid the excessive specialization encouraged by our educational system has almost precluded such a holistic approach. Specialization, for example, has prevented our understanding the way in which the various forms of mass-culture – advertising, television, radio, newspapers, magazines, pop music, paperbacks – are permeated by certain common assumptions and constitute a single, if highly complex, structure.

In this essay I intend to sketch a theory which will clarify the tasks teachers face and offer a framework in which the various forms of mass-culture can be placed for closer scrutiny and study. Finally, I will present the case for a more expressive form of education, and argue that the school should become a cultural centre for the surrounding community.

What I will try to show is this: that in the Western technocracies there has developed a sharp split between knowledge and feeling, between technique and teleology, between objective fact and personal culture. It is true that this split is a very old one and, at the theoretical level, runs through much of the Western philosophical tradition from the time of Plato; but, at the same time, it was not till after industrialization and compulsory mass-education that the split became socially incarnated and became the destiny of the vast mass of people. I have provided some of the historical analysis in the previous essays, but if we examine our own contemporary institutions and our dominant cultural forms, we will find this split expressed in nearly every aspect of our lives. If we look at education and mass-culture we find precisely this appalling division, for we see, on analysis, that schools promote the mastery of pure knowledge and pure technique with little sustained reference to the emotional, the imaginative, the personal; and that, on the other hand, mass-culture addresses itself solely to the emotional, often in its two corrupt forms of sentiment and sensation. On the one side, objectivity cut off from feeling and conscience. On the other, a raw and exploited subjectivity cut off from critical reflection and understanding. A schizophrenia, a pathology of consciousness, built into our society.

I showed earlier* how the intelligent adolescent divided his academic work from his cultural life, and felt compelled to do so. In this way his reason became identified with school and his emotions with the mass-produced artefacts (pop music, teenage magazines, advertising, Smith's paperbacks) of commercial culture. But what happens to the less able, or even the average, adolescent? He doesn't find his identity confirmed in the abstract concerns of the schools – and so comes to identify himself largely with the counterfeit culture which surrounds him, and appears to be made for him. This he feels is his culture – expressing the very rhythms of his own adoles-

*See the second essay, pp. 30 and 31.

cent experience. If there is a conflict between the powers of education and the powers of mass-culture, there can be little doubt that mass-culture exerts the greater force, because it appeals directly to the strong, undirected and unexplored feelings of the adolescent. But, in fact, there is little open conflict because the majority of teachers regard the division between the cognitive and the affective as normal, and the stark separation of the two realms as somehow inevitable. As a result, the vast majority of adolescents in the West are educated not by the schools but by the copywriters, the disc-jockeys, the hack journalists, the pop stars, the TV personalities and the invisible oligarchy of promoters and directors, manipulating the proceedings from behind the scenes. And this is nothing short of tragic, for the young form tomorrow's world.

I ought, perhaps, to define this word mass-culture a little more closely. By mass-culture I refer, in large measure, to what is commonly called 'pop-culture'. But 'pop-culture' is an ambiguous concept, for although the culture may be popular, it is not – manifestly not – made by the people, nor does it embody the actual experiences of a living people. There are virtually no 'pop' artefacts expressing the most common experience in people's lives, the experience of work. There is no celebration of work; no exploration, no protest about work. There is only silence. There are no pop artefacts defining the universal dramatic events of human life, birth, marriage, death. On these matters, the unifying preoccupations of nearly all traditional cultures, silence again. In fact, we find silence on almost every issue, political, social, religious, existential, except adolescent love conceived in an infantile manner. Let us consider, for a single moment, a true culture of the people as it exists in a pre-industrial society and we will immediately perceive the paucity and artificiality of so-called 'pop culture'. This is a description of the place of dance in Nigerian village communities:

> African village dance is what European dance might once have been – an expression of every important stage and event in the life of the individual and the entire society. There are dances for childhood and for old age, for every deity, for every major task. The overall style of dancing unifies and identifies the society because every tribe has its own style of dance.[54]

The anthropologist Stanley Diamond has defined the function of symbol-making in primitive societies as follows:

> In primitive society, the ritual drama is a culturally comprehensive vehicle for group and individual expression at critical junctures in the social round or personal life style. . . . In such ceremonies, art, religion and daily life fuse and cultural meanings are renewed and re-created on a stage as wide as life itself. . . .
>
> These rituals are also creative in the dramatic revelation of symbols and the articulation and elaboration of new roles for individuals. They make meanings explicit and renew the vitality of the group.[55]

Pop culture does not belong to people in this way – it is housed in the machine, it is manufactured in cities and distributed across provinces, and is there to secure investment and profits and, after that, more investment and more profits. In fact, as I argued in the previous essay, it would seem that industrial culture has only one goal, the increase of profits, and that it is therefore a culture dangerously out of control, without any inner moral check or purpose. All traditional cultures have been related to real needs or to some concept of universal order; industrial culture, lacking any real concept of order, rushes forward, whatever the harmful effects, whatever the human sacrifices.

By mass-culture I refer, then, to the manufacturing of culture as a commodity on a massive scale to mass markets for massive profits. In nearly all its aspects it contrasts with traditional and primitive cultures where culture is the direct expression of the individual-in-the-community and the community-in-the-individual.

How is it that mass-culture is so powerful? I have suggested that part of its formidable influence is related to the fact that it addresses itself directly, almost savagely, to the emotional and the dramatic. This is obviously true, but it is not an adequate explanation. We need a more comprehensive theory, and I think it can be partly found in the theory of mimesis, which puts at the centre of human action the desire to emulate, to 'act out' personally, whatever seems of most importance in the surrounding environment. Not through instinct but through the prolonged imitation of cultural forms man becomes human. The extraordinary power of mimesis belongs almost uniquely to human-kind. It is an inherent part of man's nature. If we look at man in a schematic and abstract way we see two things: *potentiality for becoming** and *a marked ability to imitate*. The former has been described well by a number of Existentialist philosophers who see in man an enduring problem of choice, of what to become. The Spanish Existentialist Ortega y Gasset put it like this: 'Life is our reaction to the basic insecurity which constitutes its substance.' Man thus remains, in large measure, an open question – a question resolved only by selection and decision, each man's making of himself. Yet such a making of the self is not achieved in isolation but is deeply influenced by the models that surround the individual; and man, as I now want to suggest, has a remarkable facility for imitating and learning through imitating.

Let me give one dramatic example. Jean-Claude Armen, travelling across part of the Sahara, discovered a boy who from the age of about eight months (as far as could be told) had been brought up by a herd of gazelles. Through a complex process of mimesis, the boy had become an important member of the herd. He had acquired all the skills of the gazelle. He could run well over 50 kilometres an hour, making continuous leaps about four metres in length in the manner of the gazelle. He had developed a sharp sense of smell. Using his hands, feet, nose and scalp, he was able to relay the coded signals of the herd. A gazelle culture had entirely replaced a human culture through the mimetic process. As Jean-Claude Armen points out, the existence of well over fifty such 'wild children' have been recorded, including wolf-children, ostrich-children, bear-children, lion-children. The discoveries of these strange 'children' would seem to confirm our conception of man which asserts both his potentiality to become and his powers of imitation through which he becomes one thing. The cases also reveal another element – or rather the absence of an element, for these 'wild children' are not human because they lack those symbolic forms which culminate in consciousness, self-consciousness. The distinction of human life lies in its symbolic character. It is through the prolonged imitation and re-creation of symbolic forms that man becomes recognizably human, and it is through the power of symbolic forms that man enters into the realm of

*Within this potentiality there may well lie a latent self but I would suggest that this latent self can only find itself in and through the symbolic forms provided by culture.

the ethical, the aesthetic, the intellectual and the religious. It is therefore of the utmost importance and consequence what symbolic forms, images and examples of behaviour surround the child, the adolescent and even the adult.

It is frequently asserted, and often by those who have power in forging opinions and disseminating them through the mass-media, that pop-culture has little actual influence on life; that the violence viewed is not imitated, that the values of the TV heroes and heroines are not absorbed into the lives of those who watch, that pornography has no effect on the actions of people. Or again, it is asserted vaguely that people are free to choose and possess within themselves the criteria by which to judge and select. Our theory of mimesis casts much of the liberal and progressive ideology into doubt, and urges us not only to define the limits to permissiveness but also to ask whether mass-culture, by its very organization and ideology, could ever be anything but an energy destructive of life. We face the paradox that man's own symbolism, so vital to the elaboration and development of thought and feeling in the human species, is now working against him.

II

Some research recently conducted in England gives some support to our general conclusions derived from the theory of mimesis. Over a period of twelve years Dr Belson compared the behaviour and viewing habits of 1,565 boys (aged between 13 and 16). His conclusions were summarized like this in *The Guardian*:

> Among the boys who had watched a lot of violence on television, 7.5 per cent confessed to having engaged in serious violence themselves; 56 per cent swore or used bad language, and 18 per cent were violent in sport or play. The violence admitted to by those who watched less TV was markedly lower.
>
> The kind of programmes which the more violent boys admitted watching included The Man From UNCLE, The Saint, Danger Man, Starsky and Hutch, Cannon, The Rockford Files and similar series-type productions. Parents, he said, should stop their children watching violent programmes. Though cautious about his findings Dr Belson said that in his full report, due to be published next year, he would recommend that steps be taken urgently for a major cutback in the total amount of violence shown on television.

> The programmes most suspected of inciting violence in viewers were those in which violence seemed to be thrown in for its own sake without relevance to the plot; which featured violence of a realistic kind; in which violence was presented as being in a good cause; and Westerns.[56]

There is nothing remarkably new in Dr Belson's research discoveries.* Dr Bronfennbrenner in his study of American and Soviet children came to startlingly similar conclusions.

> In a sample of more than six hundred third graders (it was) found that the children who were rated most aggressive by their classmates were those who watched television programmes involving a high degree of violence.
>
> Yet a number of the experiments we have reviewed indicate that aggressive – and even cruel – behaviour can be induced in a person without giving him any ground for grievance, by simply allowing him to observe aggressive behaviour, purely as a bystander.[57]

And finally:

> The implications of these research findings for the impact of television on its viewers are obvious. Given the salience of violence in commercial television, including cartoons especially intended for children, there is every reason to believe that this mass-medium is playing a significant role in generating and maintaining a high level of violence in American society, including the nation's children and youth.[58]

Again and again, we find examples to support the research findings of Belson and Bronfennbrenner. But to show concern only for the violent effects of the mass-media is too limiting: we must be concerned with the perpeptual diffusion of a way of life which is empty of meaning, inherently trivial, and dependent on the habit of a voracious mass consumption of goods which now threatens to destroy the ecological pattern on which all life depends.

Confronting such a challenge, what can schools, colleges, universities do? I would like to draw towards a conclusion by making a number of suggestions. At the moment a number

*Though we must always be wary of asserting a simple casual relationship between artefact and behaviour. It is vital to avoid a reductionist position. What we need to emphasize is the power of the *total* environment of symbolic communication to influence the child both in his outer and in his inner life, two aspects of a single totality.

of schools work to encourage a critical understanding of the media, try to initiate among their pupils the practice of discrimination, of selection and evaluation. This must be done in self-defence. In fact, alert English Departments have been promoting such work since 1933, when F. R. Leavis and Denys Thompson published *Culture and Environment*, the first textbook on mass-culture. This tradition has been kept alive and been extended by Raymond Williams, David Holbrook, Fred Inglis and many others. Such work in the classroom can take many forms: it can be visual (involving the analysis of imagery), it can be ethical (evaluating the judgements implicitly or explicitly made in advertisements), it can be economic (seeing advertising as the mythology for the mass-production and mass-consumption of goods), it can be psychological (examining the way in which persuasion works and is made to work). There is an extensive literature* on the subject, and such work, ideally, calls for the collaboration between a number of Departments. The approach has to be not only descriptive but also critical. Above all (as I suggested at the beginning), such work should endeavour to locate the underlying pattern of assumptions behind the apparently diverse phenomena of mass-culture. In the final analysis, a culture can only be defined as a distinct way of life; industrial culture is no exception. Seen collectively, all of its artefacts tend to emphasize, celebrate, ritualize certain dominant values (such as mobility, acquisitiveness, envy, material success, social power) and to exclude others (such as thrift, simplicity, compassion, humility, concern for truth). It is time that we had degree courses in our major European universities exploring, across the disciplines, the strengths and pathologies of industrial culture; such courses would need to draw on philosophy, psychology, ecology, the arts, sociology, the sciences, and would eventually hammer out a further body of materials and approaches for use further down in the schools.

Certainly, there are many different traditions of critical analysis and protest which such a degree course could draw from. Approaching mass-culture as I do, from a literary and philosophical perspective, I have found in running one-term

*For a good introduction see Raymond Williams' *Communications* (Penguin). For the study of advertising see Fred Inglis' *The Imagery of Power*. For the study of pop music see Charles Parker's 'Pop Music: The Manipulated Ritual' in *The Black Rainbow*. For a general survey see Denys Thompson's *Discrimination and Popular Culture*. See also Ian Robinson's *The Survival of English*.

undergraduate contextual courses at the University of Sussex four important and quite independent sources of criticism which it is vital for students to become aware of. These schools, while seldom drawn together, are by no means mutually exclusive. More often than not, they complement rather than negate each other. Brought together, they provide a powerful and many-faceted critique of industrial culture, a critique which has been generated simultaneously within and against the consumer mass-society.

The first tradition is, of course, our own eloquent and intransigent tradition emerging within English literature at the very beginning of industrialization in the voices of Blake, Coleridge and Wordsworth. This tradition, still developing, still a vivid and coherent part of literary criticism and the teaching of English, has been adequately charted (though not without Socialist bias by Raymond Williams in *Culture and Society*. His book still provides the best introduction to the field. It is difficult to select texts from such an abundant literature, but work on a short course (and the interdisciplinary contextuals at the University of Sussex generally last only one term) could concentrate on, for example, Carlyle's brief but perspicacious essay 'Signs of the Times', on Charles Dickens' polemical novel *Hard Times*, on Matthew Arnold's uneven but influential *Culture and Anarchy* and on the eloquent lectures of William Morris. From our own century texts could be selected from the seminal criticism (all developing out of the nineteenth-century tradition of moral evaluation) of T. S. Eliot, F. R. Leavis and D. H. Lawrence.

The second tradition, still to be mined by English writers, critics and teachers, is Existentialism. As I intend to explore this movement in the next essay, I will confine my comments here to pointing out that Existentialism is an extremely diverse movement within European philosophy, and, in its nineteenth-century expression (in Kierkegaard and Nietzsche), represented an impassioned concern for the individual and for subjectivity in an age which had become pathologically obsessed with the collective and with scientific objectivity. Existentialism erupted in the nineteenth century as a febrile affirmation of the category of the individual. Kierkegaard and Nietzsche envisaged the mass-society of our own times, and were among the first philosophers to declare war on it. In the context of the examination of industrial culture Kierkegaard's *The Present Age* and Ortega y

Gasset's *The Revolt of the Masses* form short but indispensable books for an understanding of the Existentialist critique.

The third tradition is found in a rather different stream of philosophy, in the post-Kantian Philosophy of Symbolic Forms developed in Ernst Cassirer's work and extended, to include the arts, in the writings of Susanne Langer. For Cassirer and Langer man's power to symbolize is the central clue to understanding his consciousness. The ability to make culture is seen as the distinguishing mark of man, taking him beyond the closed zoological order and giving him, as it were, entry into the dimension of meaning. For a full understanding of Cassirer's premise – a premise on which I believe, one can build a most illuminating critique of the symbolic forms of industrialism – one must turn to his own introductory book *An Essay on Man* and to Susanne Langer's *Philosophy in a New Key*. However, although Susanne Langer often mentions the impoverishment of expressive symbolism in industrial societies, the symbolic philosophers never critically examined the actual symbolic forms of industrial society. Here their philosophy, brought into relationship with the other traditions, is given a further importance and a greater range.

The fourth tradition, providing an important economic dimension to the criticism of industrialism, is the Frankfurt School, which consciously set out to construct a critical theory of mass-society. The Frankfurt School, adopting an essentially Marxist position, sought to answer the question 'Why hasn't the revolution happened?' Why had Marx's predictions been wrong when so much of his analysis seemed correct? What had happened to the dialectical war of opposites through which the oppressed class triumphed and came to power? The questions lead to a detailed and revised analysis of industrial society. The answer to the question seemed to lie in the fact that industrial society had the power to dissolve the dialectic, had the ability to absorb opposed principles yet without changing itself. In Marxist terms, the proletariat had been drawn into the dominant society and had come to accept alienation as reality, as its own truth. Although mass-culture was a culture of insidious and constant manipulation, the proletariat yet identified with it and experienced its counterfeit expressions as symbols of its own life. In its extraordinary ability to assimilate opposition without undergoing essential change, the consumer mass-society had secured the means, it seemed, of perpetuating itself.

The study of this process led Marcuse in his *One Dimensional Man* to analyse the symbolic forms of industrial society and the invisible tyranny they exerted. The book remains an excellent introduction to the Frankfurt post-Marxist School of philosophy and can be brought, with a certain valuable and necessary tension, into living relationship with the other three traditions of criticism.

In briefly outlining these four traditions and mentioning some of the key texts, I hope only to have given some idea of the type of work that can be done inside literature, philosophy and sociology. In any degree course these traditions would have to be studied in intimate relationship to ecological studies and studies deriving from the sciences and from technology. The work would have to be both collaborative and critical, an intelligent, sustained, profound response to the great crisis of an over-industrialized world, facing the daily possibility of its own annihilation.

But is such critical examination, though essential, sufficient, particularly at a lower level of education? Is it enough in our secondary schools to develop habits of discrimination? Does, in fact, analysis undermine the workings of the counterfeit culture outside the classroom? Or does it merely confirm the adolescent's view that schools can't possibly understand the imperatives of emotional and sensuous life? Is *the study* of mass-culture yet another expression of the schizoid split between intellect and passion? And how effectively can the arguments of reason in school be made to impinge on the appeals to the irrational made elsewhere?

I raise these questions not to undermine the study of industrial culture or its importance but in order to suggest that, if the school is to be successful, it must offer *more* than critical analysis. It must offer also forms of ritual and creative symbolism. It must attempt to create a living culture in which the young can participate and develop as responsive and responsible individuals within an encompassing community. Schools, as I have repeated throughout the course of this book, must open themselves to the subjective element and seek to work for wholeness of being, a subversive enterprise – but educational to the very core.

I argued, in an earlier essay, that society to remain both stable and vital has to embody within itself two different types of culture: one being hereditary, communal, largely unchanging;

the other being innovative, immediate, personal, experiental. They are all but opposites, but each needs the other. Like the compass points North and South, East and West, they are antithetical and complementary. In our schools, as I have implied, we have neither communal ceremony nor individual exploration. I am contending that in the light of our very pressing contemporary dilemmas, the school should move beyond critical analysis and become a centre for the development of both forms of culture. As I argued in the first section of this book, schools might become in part ceremonial centres, the places where people gather to give symbolic shape to universal experiences. But such ceremonies would not be adequate. They need, in turn, complementing by another related mode of symbolizing, which is more intimate, more personal. Here the aim of the school must be to promote among its members a fidelity to experience, and the means of expressing through all the arts the import of that experience. Schools might thus become cells of creative living.

In an age of cultural and spiritual impoverishment all the institutions of education have no choice but to become cultural centres, critical of their own society. In a muddled and distracted age, an age in which culture has deteriorated into a commodity, they must fashion, as best they can, honest and creative forms of symbolization, forms which promise to heal the division between thought and feeling described at the beginning of this essay, forms which suggest the outlines of a new integration of man. If such a critical and creative concept of education was widely adopted and put into practice, it might just be possible for education to have a deeper and greater effect than mass-culture, and that would be a beginning of that transformation of consciousness which our contemporary plight requires. Existing realities speak out against such a hope – but without some such hope, there can be no change.

On Existential Philosophy and the Practice of Education

Everywhere it is decisively concluded that thought is the highest stage of human development; philosophy moves farther and farther away from contact with primitive existential impressions and there is nothing left to explore, nothing to experience. Everything has been finished, and speculative thought has now to rubricate, classify and methodically arrange the various concepts. One does not live any more, one does not act, one does not believe.

SØREN KIERKEGAARD

FIVE

An Existential Approach to Education

We are creatures of this sort, and we are lost if we relinquish our orientation to the dry land. But we are not content to remain there. That is why our flutterings are so uncertain and perhaps so absurd to those who sit secure and content on dry land, and are intelligible only to those who have been seized by the same unrest. For them the world is a point of departure for that flight upon which everything depends, which each man must venture on his own though in common with other men, and which can never become the object of any doctrine.

KARL JASPERS

I

In this essay I have three main intentions: I want to evoke, through an autobiographical account, the barrenness of twentieth-century Anglo-Saxon philosophy; I want to outline what with misgivings I must call the Existentialist tradition in philosophy; and, lastly, I want to present an existential concept of education where the emphasis falls constantly on creative process rather than on product or measurable performance. This is an enormous task, and I have few illusions about the limitations of the essay. To be specific; I will do no justice to any one of the philosophers I mention – it isn't possible in such a short space. I will draw on what I need for my argument and, reluctantly, discard the rest. I will hurry over vast issues. I will resolve little. These limitations are all but inevitable, for it is unreal to think that in a single essay one can fully represent a swiftly moving and many-faceted stream of subversive philosophy, let alone work out its implications for educational practice. All I can hope to do is to offer a crude map, scrawling in the major landmarks and some of the possible routes into the hinterland. I take heart in the fact that for the existential philosopher meaning cannot, even at the most opportune moments, be passively transmitted but must always be actively re-created and struggled for within the consciousness of each individual. No man can educate another. He can only hope, by the example of his own manner of enquiry, to stimulate a comparable, though never identical, intellectual, aesthetic, moral or religious passion in the other. He can also provide some of the working tools and point to the perennial sources. But only the subject himself can become the agent of his own education, for education is above all an inward state of mind, a way of being-in-the-world, a desire to find and re-create meaning. Thus, as I argued in the opening essay, 'education' and 'schooling' can refer, and often do refer, to antithetical activities.

Paradoxically, the very limitations of the essay may constitute a sort of strength. Having a rough map and the invitation to embark, the reader must be responsible for making his own distinct journey into the territory. But then, it would be too easy to leave the metaphor of travel and adventure on this light note – partly because the metaphor has become, in an age of easy mobility, trite and partly because, even if we accept the metaphor, we must add that the journey is not without its dangers, and can be thoroughly problematic. Nietzsche saw with clairvoyant precision the nightmare of our own century, an age in which all received moralities and metaphysics had become uncertain, an age of crass and mass hedonism (on the one side) and a furious nihilism (on the other side). We no longer know what we value, what to live by, who we should become. There are no common traditions concerning meaning. No common centre. The landscape we are invited to cross by the Existentialists has no accompanying brochure; it resembles a ruined city, bristling with unexploded mines, with all signposts pulled up or defaced. The invitation is not a comfortable one – the philosophers I am going to discuss did not lead comfortable lives, and nor are the immediate prospects comfortable. Existentialist philosophy would have us engage with problems which are so fundamental, so acute, so disturbing, so at the very centre of our existence that, in self-defence, many have claimed that existential philosophy is not respectable, not academic, not verifiable, in short not philosophy at all. The criticisms are correct: existential philosophy is not respectable, not academic, not verifiable in a sicentific manner, but the conclusion is false. For any thinking, any verbal symbolizing which attempts to locate *meaning* and is preoccupied with such categories as 'freedom', 'authenticity'/'inauthenticity', 'being' and 'becoming', is philosophical to the marrow. To accept, as has been the Anglo-Saxon habit, a philosophy of science and a philosophy of linguistic analysis and (with uncertainty) a philosophy of morals, but to refuse a *philosophy of existence* strikes me as not only narrow but deeply and scandalously unphilosophical. It is for this reason that I want to turn my attention first to the intellectual climate in this country, a climate which has been so hostile to Existential philosophy and which, even now, still excludes it from most degree courses in philosophy. I have decided to indicate the poverty of Logical Positivism and its offspring in the most immediate manner, through a description of my own experience studying philosophy in a joint degree at an English university during the early 60's.

II

In 1961 I went up to Bristol University to study what was described as the joint school of Philosophy and English. It wasn't long before I realized that the description was wholly misleading – for there was no joint school, only two departments, each completely isolated from the other. Students wishing to succeed had to become intellectual schizophrenics; they had to learn to inhabit two disjointed domains; they had to acquire the skill of being able to master and keep separate two different modes of language and two distinct schemes of reference. In the Philosophy Department it was '*p* hook *q*' and 'what *x* seems to be saying is . . .', while in the English department it was 'moral significance', 'living tradition', 'felt life'. Providing the student adapted, providing he could keep separate the two schemata and did not seek unity of understanding, there was no immediate problem. But if he failed in this, if he sought to join what had been broken asunder, then he had to endure constant frustration and bewilderment.

In one apocryphal philosophy seminar a student attempted to articulate the foundations of her religious belief. Naively, she declared to the Oxford philosopher, 'I know because I feel it in my heart.' Such a proposition, in such a context, might well have secured the sympathy of a Pascal or a Kierkegaard, but not the twentieth-century English philosopher on the other side of the table. There was a palpable pause. The students waited. Then came the clinical reply, 'In which ventricle, may I ask?'

The remark, in the manner of the Oxford tradition, was curt, offensive and completely reductive. The brief philosophical manifesto of the student and the experience which it incarnated was dismissed, never to be offered again. Students had to learn quickly which problems and question must never be placed on the philosophical counter. It seemed that a thin-lipped disdain for existential issues had been assiduously cultivated by our mentors. Their sharp responses expelled certain ideas and conceptions even before we could adequately formulate them. Looking back, I cannot help feeling that the hard-edged system with its guarded utterances, its brittle rejections of the emotional and existential, was designed to block at source the pre-conceptual streams of philosophical speculation, and in so doing to perpetuate the Positivist status quo for ever. Any personal quest for meaning – or, if I may use a word which it would have been impossible to seriously utter then – wisdom, had to be briskly eradicated like a dangerous and contagious disease. Any existential search for wholeness was dubbed 'religious' and left at that. Thus, from the very outset, we were disqualified from generating our own philosophical ideas. We were never allowed to dissolve the thing called philosophy into the engaging personal process of philosophizing. We were never allowed to convert the inert noun into a living participle.

It is possible to grasp the failing of any body of doctrine by considering not what it contains but what it excludes, both what it chooses to leave out and what it unconsciously leaves out. I have implied that the Oxford philosophers (in their outpost at Bristol) ignored the irreducible existential core of knowledge – they did not perceive the necessary relationship between thought and the individual thinker, the essential relationship between philosophy and autobiography. They did not, could not, see that the noun knowledge is shorthand for a form of knowing, and that knowing is in turn a mode of being-in-the-world. 'A man', as Nietzsche claimed, 'may stretch himself out ever so far with his knowledge; he may seem to himself ever so objective, but eventually he realises nothing therefrom but his own biography.' Not only were we discouraged from discovering the existential roots of philosophy, we were not at liberty to read the alternative traditions of philosophical discourse, some of which proclaimed such a view. Philosophers in the Existentialist, Thomist, Marxist, Idealistic and Phenomenological movements went unread and unrecorded. There was no reference to Aquinas, to Pascal, to Hegel, to Marx, to Husserl, to name but a few of the philosophers who had been quietly pushed into the dark. To raise the name of an Existentialist was to procure the instant rejection, 'Ah! Non-philosophy!'

The Positivists had dissolved the inherited traditions of speculation and drawn up a new and simple map. According to the new model, philosophy began, effectively with Locke, ran through Hume and Bentham and Mill and from there to A. J. Ayer and Bertrand Russell. True, we glanced at Plato – to dismiss him. True, we glanced at Descartes and the Rationalists – to learn the fallacies of the ontological argument. We moved fleetingly back only to be triumphantly swept forward to the climax of twentieth-century Oxford philosophy. I look back and am scandalized by the intellectual provincialism which informed our studies.

Basically, we were taught one crude instrument for evaluation. An assertion was either verifiable or unverifiable. If it was verifiable, then it could be established by empirical procedure as being true or false. If the assertion was unverifiable, then it was classified as 'emotive'. An ethical, aesthetic or religious assertion was akin to 'Mars Bar – I like' or 'I don't like.' A commitment to this analytical tool confined philosophy to the role of clarifying linguistic utterances. The philosopher became, in effect, a language technician. Even more narrowing, however, was the assumption that only coherence and intellectual meaning could be given to statements of pure fact. This meant that the confused mass of judgements, preoccupations, intuitions, questions, fantasies, feelings – indeed, all but the sum total of human experience – could not be brought under the light of critical scrutiny and philosophical understanding. The Oxford philosophers had secured an insulated world where they could operate with some efficiency, but in so doing they had cut themselves off from the primary source of philosophical reflection, the experiencing subject, the individual in whom thought and feeling, question and apprehension, answer and doubt, run together. Philosophy was 'out there', safely removed from life's turmoil, anxieties, aspirations.

Whatever issues the more thoughtful students wanted to raise, they were condemned as 'non-philosophical'. For me, the Department was founded on negation. Broad expectations were cut down with the machinery of sneers and disdain. Some of us had come seeking seminal minds, ready to submit ourselves for a time before rich and superior intellects. This hope, this barely articulated desire, was out of all proportion to the mundane reality. We should have come not as seekers, but as engineers, blind to the problem of purposes, wanting only basic techniques and working tactics. We should have come as Philistines. Yet no-one had informed us that the disciplined love of wisdom had become, in our own time, in our own century, an ingrown academic specialism, a modest adjunct to Science.

Sitting calmly in a small room, trying to think of something that might bear on the problem of whether unicorns existed or not, it was impossible to believe that outside, for want of philosophical vision and moral concern, the world was moving inexorably to the edge of things. The unreality of our discussions blurred our minds and muffled the universe.

Yet it should not have been difficult for us to find an analogue for our own situation. Hadn't the declining Scholastics endlessly argued about how many angels could rest on a pin while the first rumblings of the Reformation disturbed the air? Were we, all unwittingly, witnessing the end of another philosophical tradition which, withdrawn from the needs of its own time, was hardening into predictable mannerism and empty convention? Perhaps there was good reason for our supposing that there might be other traditions of philosophical reflection which possessed some of the disturbed passion, introspective acuity and shafts of wisdom we were thirsty for. Was Existentialism, with its emphasis on the personal, in part, a protest against the dessication and fragmentation of knowledge? A protest against the professionalization of philosophy? Was Existentialism a return to the bright sources of human questioning? I think, as I now intend to show, it was, in many ways, all of these things. Like the Romantic Movement – to which in sensibility it is intimately related – the Existentialism which emerged through the writings of Kierkegaard and Nietzsche in the nineteenth century was a passionate response to the industrial revolution and the philosophy of mechanism which underpinned that revolution. It was a bid to draw philosophy back into existence. I want now to provide a sketch of the Existentialist tradition. I will begin by making a number of important qualifications about the concept 'Existentialism', for, unfortunately, the very word tends to deny the import of the philosophy.

III

The problem with the word 'Existentialism' is that it suggests coherence, an ordered system which claims to make sense of life. If, for example, we consider other words with the suffix 'ism' on the end – Behaviourism, Marxism, Calvinism – it can be seen that they presuppose a framework of interpretation, explanatory, interlocking, complete. If we refer to Marxism, we immediately recall the key theory of Marx which claimed that the whole anatomy of social and personal life can be discerned in the particular organization of the economy; if we refer to Calvinism we call to mind the theory of predestination, of the powers of God over and above the powers of individual will. But if we refer to Existentialism I do not think we call to mind any immediate *content*. We can point to Christian Existentialists, atheist Existentialists, agnostic Existentialists; we can point to Left-wing Existentialists and we can point to Right-wing Existentialists and to those who seem, initially, to be a-political and even anti-political. For although Existentialism provides a broad mode of philosophizing, a philosophizing within existence, it does not offer a system. In fact, Existential philosophers have been deeply suspicious of total systems and the consolations and the temptations they offer; in particular, the temptation they offer to distort experience to match the requirements of the system. Systems, by their very nature, tend to promote a false consciousness. Kierkegaard's philosophy emerged out of a fierce, almost perverse reaction to the system-building of Hegel, a system-building which Kierkegaard declared threatened to destroy the anguish, delight and meaning of individual experience. Against the over-arching rational system – a system which boldly endeavoured to explain every fragment of life in terms of an analytical and rational whole – Kierkegaard asserted the confused, paradoxical and for ever unpredictable actuality of experience. Towards the end of his life he wrote:

> If I were to desire an inscription for my tombstone, I should desire none other than 'That Individual' – if that is not now understood, it surely will be.[59]

> (I) aimed a blow at the system with the category of 'the individual'.[60]

> With the category of the individual is bound up any importance I may have.[61]

Kierkegaard sought to break the system, so that the waters from the personal and primordial springs of philosophical enquiry could seep through.

Dostoevsky, whom Nietzsche admired greatly, was making a similar protest against high reason in his *Notes from the Underground* or, as we would say, notes from the unconscious. There, in that strange short story, Dostoevsky presents the existential case with powerful economy:

> But reason is only reason, and it can only satisfy the reasoning ability of man, whereas volition is a manifestation of the whole of life, I mean, of the whole of human life, including reason with all its concomitant head-scratchings. And although our life, thus manifested, very often turns out to be a sorry business, it is life nonetheless and not merely extractions of square roots. . . . Twice-two-makes-four is not life, gentlemen. It is the beginning of death. . . .[62]

It is, I think, no accident that some of the writings of the Existentialists are fragmentary in character. Pascal's great book *Pensées* remains like a magnificent ruin, a mass of fragments and uneven jottings which he wrote on separate sheets of paper and then slowly began to edit under twenty-seven different headings. The unfinished book we have is, consequently, very much a work in process of being shaped – and this gives it an immediate existential vitality. The thoughts still belong to an actual man; they have not been sublimated into a monolithic structure, a finished artefact. Pascal himself is the poetry of the book. It is worth noting that many of Nietzsche's most disturbing observations were written as aphorisms (partly under the influence of Pascal), shocking jabs at the truth of things. The selections from his notebook collected under *The Will to Power* forms one of the best introductions to his brilliant, manic and uneven work. Reading that book one can sense the tremendous hot lava of 'ideas' being pushed up from below with terrifying energy. The style of Existentialist literature, being fragmentary, polemical, febrile, passionate, embodies, I believe, the actual crisis in meaning and values which is the hallmark of our post-Christian technocratic society. The style also testifies, perhaps, to a particular view of existence which sees life as the problematical task of choosing and becoming rather than as something already achieved and, therefore, ready to be quietly and patiently classified. For the Existentialists, the strange and uncertain turmoil, which we call euphemistically the inner life, is not easily grasped by the critical intellect. It is, even, possible, they suggest, that there are depths to which the critical intellect cannot descend. Freud admitted that the poets had charted the unconscious before him; so had the Existentialists. St Augustine, for example, wrote in his *Autobiography*:

> I cannot totally grasp all that I am. Thus, the mind is not large enough to contain itself: but where can that part of it be which it does not contain? Is it outside itself and not within? How can it not contain itself? As this question struck me, I was overcome with wonder and almost stupor. Here are men going afar to marvel at the heights of mountains, the mighty waves of the sea, the long courses of great rivers, the vastness of the ocean, the movements in the stars, yet leaving themselves unnoticed . . .*[63]

Passages with a similar import can be found in Pascal, Kierkegaard and Nietzsche.

My central point is that Existentialism does not offer a systematic theory, an enclosed and explanatory system. It is a crucial point, having not only a negative aspect but also a positive thrust. A glance at the etymology of the word *existence* reveals why. The word, deriving from the Latin *ex-sistere*, means, quite literally, *to stand out, to emerge, to become visible, to become manifest*. To exist is synonymous with *to stand forth*, to emerge from all that surrounds one in order to become a most particular person. The etymology of the word points unambiguously to the dramatic and dynamic nature of existence. To exist implies a stepping out of one's background in order to become who one is. One may, for example, be a member of a particular social class, of a particular country, of a particular family. All these details make up, as we say, 'our background' – and, as I have argued in the middle section of this book, they assert a tremendous pressure on the way we perceive and interpret the world – but they do not coincide

*This passage represents, in fact, a characteristic piece of Existential philosophizing. In it one sees the mind turning in to examine itself – one sees, therefore, the formulating of immediate questions relating to existence – and one sees the way in which responses to these questions are *paradoxical, 'the mind is not large enough to contain itself'*. One sees also the way in which *feeling runs with intellectual questioning*; that the enquiry engages *all the faculties* of the enquirer – 'As this question struck me, I was overcome with *wonder* and *almost stupor*'. The emotional energies here are not separated from the intellectual. *The philosophical action of the mind is immersed in the moving tide of life*. And finally, of course, one notices a deep preoccupation with *what is within*, a grappling with the most definite and the most mysterious of all facts, that we exist.

with our existence. *There is a sense in which a man can be said to exist only when he steps out of the background into the foreground of his own particular life*. For the Existentialist, each individual has the task of shaping his own life, of becoming his own artist. The individual, not the social system, is conceived of as the ethical, imaginative and creative agent. The burden of responsibility, or, to turn it round and see its other complementary side, the reward of creation, is thus placed with the individual and not with the system. In an age of endless bureaucracy and commercial regimentation, in an age in which the dominant revolutionary energy in the West is Marxist, and therefore preoccupied with the collective and the social cause, the existential philosopher would have us become aware of the fact that the human world can only exist in and through the consciousness of individuals. Even objectivity is an individual achievement. It is also the case that the nature of many of the academic disciplines seeking to understand man – I am thinking particularly of certain forms of sociology and psychology – seem unable to find him because by their very methodology, denying the primacy of subjectivity, they turn him into an object among other objects; they take him from his own foreground into his background and swiftly shut and lock the gates behind him. On any numerical and pseudo-empirical account, the individual is always the exception, *the unreality*, and the collective is always the norm and implicit reality. The effects of this quantitative mode of comprehension are deep, all-pervasive and quite insidious. In the nineteenth century Nietzsche complained that 'our entire sociology does not know any other instinct than that of the herd – i.e., that of the sum of zeroes, where every zero has equal rights, where it is virtuous to be zero'. In the twentieth century Martin Buber expressed the dilemma like this:

> The collectivity becomes what really exists, the person becomes derivative. . . . Thereby the immeasurable value which constitutes man is imperilled.[64]

For Buber, as for the existential philosophers, the passionate desire to exist authentically can always, at critical points, 'burst the ideological bonds of his social being'. Such authentic existence, a distinct mode of being in-the-world, cannot be quantified, cannot, without appalling reduction, be translated into computer terms or abstract data.

In brief, the 'existence' part of the concept 'Existentialism' is highly pertinent. It does hint at a major common ground between the various philosophers. But the suffix is out of tune, for the Existentialist philosophers refuse to offer the consolations of an explanatory and all-sufficing system, a refusal which, has important implications for teachers and teaching. Having made these necessary qualifications, I want now to draw up the Existentialists' line of descent.

Karl Jaspers, Martin Heidegger and, before them, Nietzsche held that the high-point in Greek philosophy may have been reached not with Socrates, as is usually claimed, but with the pre-Socratics; and that, furthermore, Socrates and Plato were responsible for creating all sorts of absolute divisions which were responsible for confusing the whole of the Western philosophical tradition. As in so many other realms, Nietzsche was the first, with characteristic rudeness and assertive energy, to claim the pre-Socratics as the true philosophers of Greece and to dismiss Socrates (whom he nevertheless admired greatly) as the villain of the piece. There is not time here to grapple with the major problems involved in such a dramatic shift in interpretation – nor am I equipped to do it. The case rests on a somewhat negative appraisal of the giants Plato and Socrates and a positive appreciation of their shadowed predecessors. What I want to try to do here is to briefly point to the powerful existential element in the Pre-Socratics. I will take Heraclitus as my example, for in the 130 fragments that remain of his work we find both a style and a content which powerfully resembles that of the Existentialists.

Heraclitus himself was aware of his oracular style, and in one of the surviving fragments wrote, 'And the Sibyl, with raving lips uttering things mirthless, undecorated and unperfumed, reaches over a thousand years with her voice, thanks to the god in her.'[65]

In another fragment he declared, 'The Lord, to whom the oracle of Delphis belongs, neither affirms nor conceals but suggests.'[66]

Ortega y Gasset, the Spanish Existentialist, has described Heraclitus' style as follows:

> Heraclitus could not write a continuous text book. He expressed his ideas in spurts, in brief pronouncements, which in their attempt each time to be total statements were stylistically compressed and a sort of doctrinal dynamite. Hence his renowned obscurity. Heraclitus'

> style therefore consists in expressing his highly individualistic being in the form of thundering pronouncements of the sort that can spout forth in any biting, 'flashing', electric conversation.[67]

In Heraclitus, critical philosophy emerges out of the mythological. In the surviving fragments one senses a personal passion for comprehension, at once *using and transforming* the traditional forms of religious incantation in a creative act of mimesis. In Heraclitus, thought and feeling have not yet separated. The understanding remains sensuous. The thought flashes forth in a series of images. We sense behind each utterance a wealth of profound, if undifferentiated, meaning. We sense a new quest, a new orientation, an emerging discipline: philosophy, in its first state, characterized by an almost arrogant exuberance and streaming intellectual vision.

Let me briefly refer to some of these conceptions, all powerfully echoing subsequent existential philosophy. First, there is the mighty conception of the universe as perpetual energy, as a constant state of becoming, without origin and without conclusion:

> This world which is the same for all, no one of gods or men has made; but it was ever, is now and ever shall be an ever-living Fire, with measures of it going out.[68]

> The sun is new every day.[69]

> You cannot step twice into the same rivers: for fresh waters are ever flowing in upon you.[70]

Then there is the further notion that this act of becoming which is our universe is held together by the tense and necessary balance of opposites:

> Homer was wrong in saying: 'Would that strife might perish from among gods and men!' He did not see that he was praying for the destruction of the universe: for, if his prayer were heard all things would pass away.[71]

> Men do not know how what is at variance agrees with itself. It is an attunement of opposite tensions, like that of the bow and the lyre.[72]

> It is the opposite which is good for us.[73]

This celebration of strife, this insistence on the essential need for contraries, on the necessity of opposites to life, runs through Existentialist philosophy like an electric current. Pascal jotted down as one of his thoughts, 'at the end of every truth we must add that we remember the opposite truth'. One of Kierkegaard's imperatives was 'work to develop the contrast'. Nietzsche claimed that one should internalize warring philosophers so that the dispute might continue in one's own mind; eventually, if one could endure the conflict, to provide the materials for a new synthesis. Rather than a simple, unambiguous, linear logic, Existentialists would urge us to develop a more subtle and dialectical logic having the power to represent within itself conflicting concepts, warring energies, contradictory states of being. At its most positive, such a dialectical logic leads to the notion of the complementarity of opposites where, as north demands south and up demands down, so self demands other, innovation demands tradition, good demands evil. I want later to define a little more closely the various meanings of this word dialectic. Certainly, it seems to me that this is the sort of logic we should be nurturing in our schools, whereas we tend to find only enclosed hierarchical systems symbolizing an utterly outdated concept of knowledge and values, as if they were somehow given on the shelves of the industrial supermarket and that all the teacher had to do was to pick them up and distribute them, as best he could, among his pupils. Our schools are two hundred years behind the metaphysical crisis which informs our age.

Finally, we discern in Heraclitus a concern for what the Existentialists have called authenticity and inauthenticity, true and false forms of being. Heraclitus, for example, noted the way in which many people fail to coincide with themselves, being 'preoccupied with becoming unpreoccupied',* endlessly moving away from the centre: 'They are estranged from that with which they have most constant intercourse.'[74]

Against this perceptive, and paradoxical, utterance, we must place an even shorter fragment which with a monumental simplicity simply asserts, 'I have sought for myself'.[75]

In handling such tiny translated fragments there is a danger – there is always the unconscious temptation to project our own meanings into them, and then to innocently draw them out as if they were actually 'out there'. Even while admitting

*To quote Ortega y Gasset's succinct formulation.

to this possibility, I would yet want to say that there is an irreducible existential element in many of these fragments – fragments in which the poetic and the philosophical are still happily intertwined. The positive re-evaluation of the Pre-Socratics by some of the Existentialists would seem to be part of a general and quite necessary return to the primitive, *a return to sources*, a return to a pristine state before various elements of the psyche became divided and dislocated, before reason was set up against feeling, before logic was set up against imagery, before the knower was sharply separated from the known, before the concept was reified and the senses neglected, before the body split from the mind. But a naive return to primitive origins is never really possible. One simply cannot shed the great load of history called Western Civilization as if it was somehow quite extraneous, somehow not part of our inmost selves. What is possible is a return to sources in order to reintegrate all the painfully diverse and disordered elements at a higher level of existence. This is what Nietzsche was attempting to do, to live through the trauma of Western Civilization in order to transcend it, in order to come through to a new unity of being, a unity of being having much in common with the ecstatic nobility of the Pre-Socratics, but different because of all that had happened since, and which had to be consciously and painfully transcended in order to reattain that position. For Kierkegaard, on the other hand, the return was a return to a faith in Christ who had been crucified a second time by his own instrument, Christianity. But, even so, Kierkegaard was still burrowing under the heap of history, in an attempt to return to sources.

Moving forward from Heraclitus, it is impossible to pass Socrates without noting a distinct existential element in his philosophizing. Kierkegaard wrote his dissertation on Socrates, and conceived of him as the highest form of philosophical existence. He admired the way in which Socrates lived his philosophy with an extraordinary passion and a compelling inwardness. In Plato's *Apologia* we hear Socrates addressing the court which found him guilty of corrupting the young and not worshipping the Gods recognized by the state, and which exacted the penalty of death:

> It is literally true (even if it sounds rather comical) that God has specially appointed me to this city, as though it were a large thoroughbred horse which because of its great size is inclined to be lazy and needs the stimu-

> lation of some stinging fly. It seems to me that God has attached me to this city to perform the office of such a fly; and all day long I never cease to settle here, there, and everywhere, rousing, persuading, reproving every one of you. You will not easily find another like me, gentlemen, and if you take my advice you will spare my life. I suspect, however, that before long you will awake from your drowsing, and in your annoyance you will take Anythus' advice and finish me off with a single slap; and then you will go on sleeping till the end of your days, unless God in his care for you sends someone to take my place.[76]

The tone is light, almost ironical, but the issues at stake are of the utmost gravity. It was no accident that Kierkegaard was drawn to Socrates, for Socrates' life was to mirror his own. Like Socrates, Kierkegaard towards the end of his life felt himself called to attack the the status quo, and died in the middle of the furore he had created.

According to Socrates, philosophy is a new way of living, a way of examining one's own life and others in order to live more truly. His commitment is wholely existential. Unlike the sophists who taught sophistry, words to impress, concepts to toy with, empty phrases for political and commercial barter, Socrates had the courage to turn his own life into an experiment in order to discover what, if anything, he could live by. So absorbed was he by the need for a moral philosophy of man – a philosophy of the good – that, according to Xenophon, he dismissed physics and theoretical mathematics as worthless. His remorseless pursuit for moral meaning and moral certainty, together with his knack of offending in the market-place those in power who wanted an untested respect from the populace, led to his death: a death he met with the same open questioning – almost a deep scientific curiosity – he brought to bear on any other event in life, large or small.

Nietzsche claimed, 'I care for a philosopher only to the extent that he is able to be an example.' Although Nietzsche attacked Socrates as 'the theoretical man' in flight from his own debauched nature, it still seems to me that he remains the great exemplar, in that he lived out his philosophy as a private mission, a high calling, not to be discarded at the order of the state or to be forsaken at the moment of death. It is fascinating to observe how Socrates under pressure, under the turmoil of doubt and difficulty, always consults his inner daimon. In this respect he is aware of a source of truth not against reason but beyond it, locked like a god within his own existence. This is a profoundly existential practice, a determination not to be estranged from what is closest to one. In this manner Socrates' life constitutes a noble example of ultimate concern and existential commitment.

Socrates is also the master of dialectics and irony – both of which Kierkegaard regarded as essential elements of any existential philosophy. His irony consists in not knowing while others, who know not, claim to know. Thus *his wisdom consists in his ignorance*. A negative achievement, one is tempted to assert, until one thinks that ignorance is the pre-condition for knowing, and, therefore, a positive stance of mind. This state of 'not knowing in existence now in order to know later' is central to Socrates' pedagogy (and I think teachers have much to learn from it). In his court speech (according to Plato's version) he defines this negative wisdom in relationship to the inevitable encounter with death:

> No one knows with regard to death whether it is not really the greatest blessing that can happen to a man; but people dread it as though they were certain that it is the greatest evil; and this ignorance, which thinks that it knows what it does not, must surely be ignorance most culpable. This, I take it, gentlemen, is the degree, and this the nature of my advantage over the rest of mankind; and if I were to claim to be wiser than my neighbour in any respect, it would be in this: that not possessing any real knowledge of what comes after death, I am also conscious that I do not possess it.[77]

Socrates' habitual confession of ignorance leads us to his concept of dialectical philosophy. I have used the word dialectic before to suggest a mode of philosophical formulation which is capable of holding within itself opposite concepts. Dialectical philosophy, in this sense, is a philosophy which assumes that reality is structured in polarities, and that one needs a double vision to grasp them. Marxism is sometimes called dialectical materialism because it conceives of history as a contending struggle of opposite classes – bourgeoisie and proletariat – which cannot be reconciled, and which through warfare leads eventually to a new synthesis, the classless state. Dialectical is used here to refer to a dynamic concept of history in which, in the same society, opposites are held precariously together, generating that energy which eventually destroys the system. Heraclitus' view is dialectical in a similar sense. So is Hegel's.

Socrates' philosophy is dialectical in a rather different sense, and in two related ways. Here the etymology of the word points us to a proper understanding. *Dialektos* in Greek means speech, discourse. Socrates, it must be remembered, never wrote a word. The philosophizing was always generated within the context of a group of people talking and listening.* Quite simply, Socrates' method was to engage people in conversation. Through a concentrated and subtle process of questioning he would then lead the participants, who began with an easy sense of what was certain or right, to a state where they too had to experience their own ignorance. Then out of the confusion, systematically engendered within the dialogue, would emerge the search for a meaning, tested at every point by rational argument. In this process Socrates claimed to act in a similar way to his mother, who was a midwife. His task was, in the first place, not to provide but to generate, to give birth to critical philosophy in the consciousness of the other. Philosophy is not an imposition of ideology but an inward liberation made possible through a sustained and collaborative examination of personal meaning. Such an approach provides one model of authentic teaching, a teaching in which nothing is taught but in which personalities can be changed for ever. It also provides us with an enduring concept of education which I invoked and defended in the first essay of this book.

The other concept of dialectics, also employed by Socrates, provides almost a bridge from the first concept of dialectic as speech to the modern concept of dialectic as the struggle of opposites. It was also Socrates' habit to encourage in conversation positions which seemed polar and mutually exclusive. This in itself created the psychic energy which could then be harnessed to go beyond both. All teachers know that a dull class is one in which everybody agrees. This is because in order to think passionately and precisely we often need to encounter an opposed conception of things; and not only in the abstract, but in the actual life of another person, and not just another person but *that person there* who is now, this moment, speaking and giving expression to an impossible, an outrageous and an authentic view of the world. It is in the warp and weft of discussion, exploring opposed conceptions, that philosophy takes wing: and for this conception of philosophy as dialogue we owe a great debt to Socrates.

*In this it is the very opposite of Heraclitus' approach, which is solitary and prophetic in character.

It is deeply ironical and therefore wholly appropriate that having praised Socrates so highly, I must now indicate why his actual philosophy, as opposed to his methods and actions, is not existential. Let me put the matter simply and bluntly. Socrates was guilty of conferring reality to abstractions. Now, as was argued in the opening essay, abstractions are essential to the free life of developing consciousness, but Socrates turned these vital concepts, evolved by man to enhance his understanding of the world in which he lived, *into essences*. In Socrates and particularly in his disciple Plato, one notices the habit of taking concepts like 'justice', 'beauty', 'good', 'truth' out of all the particular contexts in which they have a concrete meaning and conferring on them not only a universal meaning but also an actual existence. Abstract terms were thus elevated and housed in an eternal realm beyond the actual and the possible. And this in turn led inexorably to the informing notion that what strikes us as real is in fact only a shadow cast by the ideal. Furthermore, as this invisible order of ideal forms is seen as fundamentally rational in its nature, reason is seen as the highest and distinguishing faculty in man. Thus man becomes *Homo sapiens, Homo rationalis*. The senses, the feelings, the imagination, the unconscious energies which materialize in the form of dreams and fantasies, are all regarded with immense suspicion, as disruptive forces working against rational lucidity and the comprehension of the ideal. Here, in this complex tangle of powerful assumptions and beliefs, we find a number of dissociations which have vitiated Western civilization for over two thousand years: there is the dissociation between body and mind, between the real and the ideal, between time and eternity. Nietzsche, who suffered enormously from these divisions, had the perspicacity to see that 'the faith in the categories of reason is the cause of nihilism'. Because the faith in reason is no longer possible, the opposite of that faith is manifested. Nihilism is the immediate, dramatic and catastrophical reversal of what has been the dominant orientation for over two thousand years. Not idealism, but sensationalism; not the mind, but the body; not the eternal, but the fleeting instant (and under technicism the mechanization of all these things, and under commercialism the exploitation). Is it possible to characterize our age as living out such a negative relationship to the intellectual past? As an age in which all that has been excluded is being, often at a most banal and vulgar level, sought after? I think this is part of a necessary interpretation. Yet at the same time, such a reaction, infinitely complex in all its ramifications and impossible adequately to conceptualize, does not, of course, constitute a reintegration but only perpetuates the old divisions, by an *over*-emphasis on what was formerly *under*-emphasized. At its best, the existential tradition has been a passionate attempt within Western philosophy to find that lost unity of mind within body, of the ideal within the real, of eternity within time. Such a quest has inevitably entailed a fierce critique of reason as it was understood by the Greeks after the formative influence of Socrates.

This critique can be found in St Augustine's *Confessions*, though considerably less so in his formal theology. The critique of reason can be found again in the work of Pascal, who was particularly aware of the irrational nature of life and of its share contingency – 'Cleopatra's nose – if it had been shorter, the whole face of the earth would have changed.' Human life, as it is lived, never conforms to a simple geometrical pattern. Pascal, furthermore, developed a positive concept of intuition as a means of knowing, a subtle power of the mind to penetrate difficulties and to sense, immediately, fitting answers to them. In *Notes for a Preface to a Treatise on Geometry or on Logic* he wrote of intuition:

> One can barely perceive these principles, one feels rather than sees them, one has the utmost trouble in making them sensible to those who don't feel them naturally. These matters are so delicate and numerous that a very sharp, delicate apprehension is needful to feel them and judge them rightly and properly according to this feeling . . . We must see the matter all of a sudden, at a glance, not by the processes of reason . . . of course the mind is at work therein, but it works tacitly, naturally, without art. For the true statement of such matters surpasses all men's powers, and even the awareness of them is the property of only a few.*[78]

*Pascal's distinction between the rational and intuitive is given further shape in some of Nietzsche's work. The following metaphor, for example, attempts to define the differences between a rational and an intuitive approach (which Pascal often termed 'the spirit of finesse'):

> One sees in imagination two wanderers by a wild forest stream which carries with it rolling stones: the one light-footed leaps over it using the stones and swinging himself upon them even further and further, though they precipitously sink into the depths behind him. The other stands helpless there most of the time: he has first to build a pathway which will bear his heavy, weary step: sometimes that cannot be done and then no god will help him across the stream.

It is axiomatic in existential philosophy that reason alone cannot penetrate existence, that life is always more than we can rationally conceptualize.

In a short essay it is impossible to describe in any detail the thought of any one of the philosphers I have mentioned. That, however, has not been my intention. I am anxious to indicate only some of the central themes of Existentialist philosophy and to indicate the nature of the tradition. I have referred to the work of Heraclitus, Socrates, St Augustine and Pascal. I must now with the utmost brevity describe the eruption of the Existentialist spirit in the nineteenth century, the century in which many critics would argue (against my own case*) that Existentialism had its origins.

In the nineteenth century Existentialism developed as a reaction to the system-building of Hegel, a philosopher who ambitiously set out to draw all of history into an evolving whole. In 1841 Schelling gave a series of lectures to demolish Hegel. Kierkegaard attended those lectures – as did Engels, Bakunin and Burckhardt. Paul Tillich believes that the Existentialist movement in the nineteenth century began with these lectures. Kierkegaard returned to Denmark, and three years later published his *Philosophical Fragments*. It is pertinent that Engels was present at Schelling's lectures, for some of the early Marxist writings – some of them, apparently, still not published in Russia – have a strong existential flavour. In 1844 Marx and Engels, both responding to and reacting against Hegel, declared:

> History does *nothing*, possesses no enormous riches, fights no fight. Much rather it is Man – real living man – who does everything and both possesses and fights. It is not 'history' that employs man to carry out its ends, as if it were a person apart; history is *nothing* but the activity of man pursuing his own ends.[79]

We are not, in other words, the passive victims of an inevitable process but active creators of meanings and ends. We not only reflect, we also express. Reality is not given, it is made, and as

*My own case is that Existentialism is best seen as a mood and mode of philosophizing. It exists where there is a profound and genuine attempt to ground philosophy in existence. For this reason I find Maurice Friedman's anthology *The Worlds of Existentialism*, which includes Heraclitus, parts of the *Old* and *New Testament*, Eckhart, Boehme, Pascal, *The Tales of Hasidism* as well as, for example, Sartre and Heidegger, both congenial and more comprehensive than Walter Kaufmann's symposium *Existentialism: from Dostoevsky to Sartre.*

Kierkegaard would insert here, it is made only by *the individual*. Marx later succumbed to system-building and, alas, historical process once again was elevated, with a materialist base, to explain man's every action.

Nietzsche, the most disturbing philosopher in the whole of the Western tradition, was born in 1844, eleven years before the death of Kierkegaard. Nietzsche's writings provide an inexhaustible source of philosophical theory and psychological insight. Many of the major movements of our own century are prefigured in his writing. Frequently his insights are left undeveloped, yet they are so pointed that they penetrate to the very axis of reality. Many of his insights could provide – have, in fact, provided – the legitimate area for a lifetime's exploration. There is a real sense in which psycho-analysis began with Nietzsche and not with Freud. It was Nietzsche who asserted that 'the power of moral prejudices had penetrated deep into the most spiritual world', there acting 'in a harmful, inhibiting, blinding, distorting fashion'. And claimed, 'For psychology is now once again the road to the fundamental problem'.

It was Nietzsche who anticipated the central hypothesis of the symbolic philosophers. In *Beyond Good and Evil* he made the claim that we read the world more through our symbols than through our senses. He suggests that much of our thinking is dominated by grammatical functions, remarking that *any specific language opens up certain possibilities of world-interpretation and closes others*. Driving this insight even further, Nietzsche claims:

> It is we alone who have fabricated causes, succession, reciprocity, relativity, compulsion, number, law, freedom, motive, purpose: and when we falsely introduce this world of symbols into things . . . we once more behave as we have always behaved, *mythologically*.[80]

Thus, according to Nietzsche, science is also a mythology, a projection of categories upon the face of the unknown.

These examples suggest, I hope, something of the disturbing profundity of Nietzsche's thought. His thinking remains wholly modern. At the centre of Nietzsche's philosophy lies his conviction that God is dead:

'Is not the greatness of this deed [man's denial of God] too great for us?' he asks. 'Must not we ourselves become Gods simply to seem worthy of it?' Nietzsche's own life was a courageous, if disastrous, attempt to confront the trauma which must follow upon the collapse of any great unifying religion. His work was an attempt to confront the trauma and to go beyond it. His life ended in madness.

In contrast, Kierkegaard sought to renew Christianity, which he believed had betrayed Christ – hence his *Attack on Christendom.* Kierkegaard sought a unique relationship to God in the leap of faith, outside of all ministries and social bodies, and in defiance of his age. Yet for all their immense strengths, both Kierkegaard and Nietzsche lack understanding of the formative power of relationships and of the deep and legitimate need for community. They offer us great but perhaps necessarily partial insights. Their work is radically incomplete – notes scrawled and placed in bottles and sent out to sea in the hope that at another time their messages might be received and understood. We know the hope was not unjustified.

It is a paradox, but the tragic and broken figures of Nietzsche and Kierkegaard have much to tell us about unity of being. They remind us that philosophy should never become too far removed from the problems of existence, and that philosophy must become again a matter of man, individuals in the actual world, passionately seeking (though perhaps never finding) wholeness of meaning, wholeness of being. Indeed, this demand constitutes the major challenge of Existentialism: a challenge which a number of disciplines, in our own century, have met. Modern theology, given shape in the writings of Tillich, Bonhoeffer, Barth and Bultmann, is permeated by existential concepts and preoccupations. So is modern psychotherapy; the work of Binswanger, Frankl, Rollo May and R. D. Laing is thoroughly existential in character, asserting the desire for meaning as the primary need in human life and relationship. Even a significant number of sociologists have adopted a phenomenological approach*, and found it infinitely more productive than the conventional approach of quantifying 'data' through various forms of statistical analysis. Yet in the field of education there has been a virtual silence, an unwillingness to grapple with the Existentialist tradition and to relate its insights

*Phenomenology as a special method of knowing was developed by William Dilthey (1833-1911), by Husserl (1859-1938) and by Merleau-Ponty (1907-61). It represents an attempt to find a fitting way of studying human experience not derived from naturalistic science. It sought to develop the art of observing human phenomena without projecting preconceptions. A recent practical application of the method can be seen in R. D. Laing's and Aaron Esterson's *Families of Schizophrenics.*

to the tasks of education. What would an existential concept of education look like? What qualities would it emphasize? How would such a concept relate to present practice? These are difficult questions to answer. Each philospher would meet the questions with his own distinct emphases. Sartre, for example, would emphasize the freedom of the individual; Martin Buber the power of relationship and the place of the community. The philosophies I have referred to in this essay cannot be melted down and recast as a single theory. Yet, at the same time, there are certain informing assumptions, certain principles which allow us to see the various philosophies as forming a somewhat elusive but undeniable tradition. What I will try to do is to give, in a personal matter, a description of education based on these unifying characteristics.

IV

It would seem consistent with an Existentialist approach to philosophy to conceive of education not so much as the set movement of the learner towards explicit ends as an indivisible process in which the individual is completely engaged, a process in which the individual is struggling to give form, character and meaning to the act of living itself. In an important sense, this could also be called an aesthetic concept of education because it views the individual not so much as a passive learner but more as a maker, a creator, an artist. It is unfortunate that grammar compels us to use the word 'education' as a noun, as if it was an object 'out there', fixed and unchanging. We talk about people who have been given 'a good education', as if education was a tangible something which can be quite simply conferred on fortunate individuals. Grammar and popular usage alike conspire to conceal the elusive, dramatic and subjective nature of education, truly conceived. For education, interpreted according to existential philosophy, is not merely an acquisition, not a collection of certificates, not an immobile knowledge about the world; it is rather the very act of consciousness struggling for adequacy of understanding and expressive existence. Education is that in which I am wholly involved, the continuous effort to re-create myself within the context in which I exist. Really, we need a verb or participle to indicate the nature of education – for to talk about it as an object among other objects (like insurance, employment, entertainment) is, as I argued more fully in the first essay, to misconstrue the immense import of the concept.

The poet Coleridge, wanting to establish a personal concept of education, suggested somewhere that we should discard the word 'knowledge' and insert in its place 'growledge'. Even more than the word education, the word knowledge suggests by its clean-cut, object-pointing nature a world of ordered facts outside of all human consciousness; facts which are unambiguously 'there', simply to be assimilated by the knower. The grammar once again misleads, for it urges us unwittingly to reify knowledge, to elevate it above the process of knowing, to put it outside on the other side of existence, when on reflection we can quickly discern that knowledge can only belong within consciousness, and, therefore, within all the uncertainties, ambiguities, fluctuations and fallibilities of consciousness. To put it in its most economic form, *there can be no knowledge without knowers, and knowers in turn must, on analysis, dissolve into a multitude of individuals living in quite specific contexts, relationships and cultures.* We have tended since at least the time of the Renaissance to divorce knowing from being, the objective from the subjective, the conclusion from the process of enquiry. What Coleridge was demanding by the exchange of 'growledge' for 'knowledge' was a swift return to a more integrated concept of man in which the search for understanding, in the form of the sciences, the humanities and the arts, was comprehended as a movement *from within outwards*, an unfolding and progressive articulation of the self in relationship to the world which surrounded it: in brief, he was calling for a profound reintegration of knowing and existing.

Writing at roughly the same time as Coleridge, Kierkegaard was likewise committed to showing how the development of pure objectivity had dramatically eclipsed the most immediate and primary sense of being alive as a distinct person, of existing here-and-now.

> Everywhere it is decisively concluded that thought is the highest stage of human development; philosophy moves farther and farther away from existential impressions and there is nothing left to explore, nothing to experience. Everything has been finished, and speculative thought has now to rubricate, classify and methodically arrange the various concepts. One does not live any more, one does not act, one does not believe.[81]

The expansion of knowledge about the world, inspired by scientific discovery and directed by scientific theory, seemed to lie over and against the individual, making him experience his unique existence as superfluous. 'The way of objective reflection', wrote Kierkegaard, 'makes the subject accidental and thereby transforms existence into something indifferent, something vanishing. Away from the subject the objective way of reflection leads to the objective truth and while the subject and his subjectivity become indifferent, the truth also becomes indifferent, and this indifference is precisely its objective validity; for all interest, like all decisiveness, is rooted in subjectivity.'

The pursuit of objective knowledge, knowledge about the world, leads to a loss of inwardness and a paralysing dissociation between 'self' and 'other'. It is illuminating to place against Kierkegaard's analysis an excerpt from Darwin's *Autobiography* where he reveals the narrowing and dulling effects of scientific investigation on his own being:

> But for many years I cannot endure to read a line of poetry: I have tried lately to read Shakespeare, and found it so intolerably dull that it nauseated me. I have also lost almost any taste for pictures or music. . . . My mind seems to have become a kind of machine for grinding general laws out of large collections of fact, but why this should have caused the atrophy of that part of the brain alone, on which the higher tastes depend, I cannot conceive. . . . The loss of these tastes is a loss of happiness, and may possibly be injurious to the intellect, and more probably to the moral character, by enfeebling the emotional part of our nature.[82]

The obsession for the general and the abstract, the endless sifting of endless facts, worked directly against the development of inward life. 'Objective reflection makes the subject incidental' and makes our own existence, our own quite unique presence in the world 'something indifferent, something vanishing'. And if this was true of such an original and pioneering scientist as Darwin, how much more true is it of all the pupils in our schools who are not even asked to sift the facts but merely to record them, to memorize them and to dutifully return them! Schools labour incessantly on convergent problems, problems where the answers are already given in the back of the book. All the evidence we have would seem to show that our educational system, faithfully embodying a mechanistic 17th/18th/19th Century concept of knowledge, becomes, as soon as the child leaves nursery school, progressively more abstract and cognitive. Education in the limited form of schooling can thus be interpreted as *a systematic flight from existence*; an attempt to blot out the dirty smudge of the self so as to secure 'pure objectivity' and 'final neutrality'. Such a system has inevitably culminated in a society which possesses an exquisitely refined technology devoid of reference to truly human purposes, and a barbaric culture, amorphous, hedonistic and unbelievably banal. All the energies that traditional cultures have lavished on the fabrication of self have been transferred to the impersonal machine which has now reached an acme of refinement (as, for example, in the technology necessary for air travel, for heart transplants, for nuclear warfare) and the inner life, the basic material of all religious and aesthetic disciplines in the past, has been left in a raw inchoate state, fed with the cheapest products, the paltriest of conceptions, the crudest of 'stimuli'. To say that a civilization grounded in such a dissociation between technology and inward culture, science and conscience, object and subject, must, unless it radically changes, destroy itself is almost to utter a platitude; yet once again it must be said. And said not to be destructive, but in order to ask the further questions 'what can be put against it? What can be developed that points away from Faustian technocratic civilization, that points beyond it?' The questions are momentous. I will try to respond to them by making more explicit my opening remarks on education as process.

Existentialists would have us develop a concept of wholeness, of an education committed to the simultaneous development of the emotional, sensory, intellectual and imaginative faculties. Our educational system is pathologically abstract, obsessed with the transmission of facts, obsessed with examination results, obsessed with the classification of knowledge and children alike. We need in contrast to develop the whole person, to make him passionately intelligent and intelligently passionate. It is vital that, at fitting moments, we impregnate scientific studies with aesthetic feeling and bring a moral concern to bear upon their discoveries, that we do not remove them entirely from the philosophical question 'How do I know?' and the existential and moral question 'How can I be responsible for that which I know?' The present lack of concern for the maltreatment of animals in numerous scientific experiments, for example, points to a tragic dissociation of knowledge and conscience among scientists. In our schools the curriculum as a whole must labour for a fitting integration, for a science which is not seen as an absolute end in itself but seen as an expression of man's existence and related to his true needs and therefore to ethical constraints.

It is also important for the child *to feel* science, for him to be aesthetically delighted in the underlying patterns in nature, to sense that he is touching, and not too intrusively, upon the mystery of things, and to experience himself as part of that mystery.

Against Darwin's nineteenth-century testimony, we may assert the following remarks of Einstein made in our own century:

> I maintain that *cosmic religiousness* is the strongest and *most noble driving force* of scientific research. Only the man who can conceive the gigantic effort and above all *the devotion*, without which original scientific thought cannot succeed, can measure the *strength of feeling* from which alone such work . . . can grow.[83] (my italics)

We know that the driving force behind most contemporary scientific research is, in fact, not of this emotional and noble nature. We also know that it ought to be, and that such a fine disposition of mind can only exist on a wide scale if it is gently developed through the total curriculum established in our schools, colleges and universities.*

In the arts, which are concerned above all with the development of subjectivity, the slow clarification of existence through expressive symbolic forms, we need to develop, in relationship

*It is inevitable that these brief remarks do not convey the immense complexity of the issue at stake. It is clear that many scientific discoveries have had their origins in creative experiences comparable with the experiences which have led to the creation of works of art. These experiences have invariably been strange, moving, elusive, dramatic, emotional. In the case of the arts the embodiment of the emotion in the artefact is crucial to its value. In the sciences this is not the case: here in the defining of a principle it is crucial that the specific personal emotion of the scientist has been expunged and that the principle is stated so impersonally that it is open to test and verification over a sustained period of time. For this reason, science develops cumulatively, unlike the arts. Science as a symbolic form moves from the existential to the general, from the personal to the public. Nevertheless, it remains a construct of the mind, and therefore part of culture for which we are responsible. Also, in its origins, science stems from the same sense of wonder and curiosity about the universe which gives birth to the arts. It is vital that science (like philosophy) should return, at critical points, to the creative manifold from which it has evolved. The dialectic demands that we move not only forwards to greater differentiation of activity but also backwards to the original primordial unity.

to the concept of wholeness, coherent pedagogies and disciplines. There has developed during the last few decades a rather free and slack notion of creativity: that whatever the child splashes down on paper, or scrawls in his exercise book, is spontaneous, and therefore artistic, and to be, if not worshipped, at least unconditionally accepted, without guided criticism or exacting commentary. Any notion of the development of form, the development of skill, the development of aesthetic awareness, aesthetic discrimination has been noticeably absent. There has been a general absence of intelligent thought about what the arts might *mean* both for the full development of the child and for the curriculum as a whole. Few have considered the important cognitive elements in the arts. Few have considered the ways in which emotion, like reason, can be developed and refined. Often there has emerged a division between expression and technique, with an underlying assumption that technique is necessary only for public prose transactions and that expression is private and, necessarily, idiosyncratic and anarchic. This division has led, inexorably, to the present ignorant demand from the government 'let's get the techniques right and forget about the expression bit'. Both sides, 'the progressive' and 'the functional', would seem to overlook the fact that technique and expression are complementary concepts. How can you adequately express anything without techniques? And why should you want techniques, why should you struggle to master them, unless you actually want to express something? To inculcate techniques without continual reference to deep expressive needs is an infallible method for creating idiots.

In our schools, as in our universities, we lay too much emphasis on the final products of creative and intellectual energy. These products – systematic theories, completed works of art, historical reconstructions – often possess a dauntingly impressive order and stand over and against the individual like immovable monuments. In fact, they easily inhibit the individual's own potential for discovery, theorizing and creating, and also mask the extraordinary turmoil of energy which attended their creation. If we scrutinize the origins of great cultural artefacts we will invariably find them emerging out of a fertile chaos; stray notes, recurring images, accidental observations, floating fragments, unconscious associations. Liam Hudson in *The Cult of the Fact* wrote:

> My assumption is that human thought, before it is squeezed into its Sunday best, is a nebulous and intuitive affair, in place of logic, there brews a stew of hunch and partial insight, half submerged.[84]

It is illuminating to place against Liam Hudson's comment a remark made by D. H. Lawrence when he was in the middle of writing *The Rainbow:*

> I am doing a novel which I have never grasped. Damn its eyes, there I am at page 145, and I've no notion what it's about. I hate it. F. says it is good. But it's like a novel in a foreign language I don't know very well – I can only just make out what it is about.[85]

I suspect that any study of the creative process would confirm Liam Hudson's assumption. As Yeats, a poet deeply influenced by Nietzsche, wrote in 'The Circus Animals' Desertion', all the masterly images, casting their spell upon humanity, began in the cluttered and uncertain realm of daily consciousness, of ordinary life:

> Those masterful images because complete
> Grew in pure mind, but out of what began?
> A mound of refuse or the sweepings of a street,
> Old kettles, old bottles, and a broken can,
> Old iron, old bones, old rags, that raving slut
> Who keeps the till. Now that my ladder's gone,
> I must lie down where all the ladders start,
> In the foul rag-and-bone shop of the heart.[86]

It is tempting in an age of unparalleled banality to set culture up *against* life, but we must resist the temptation and endeavour to see culture as the manifestation of life, as beginning in man's passionate desire for existential meaning and as returning to it. Children must come to know about culture because they too are busy makers of culture; they must come to know about Science because they too are the makers of Science. We must not put subjects over and against life and the compelling needs of life.

If we are to adopt an existential philosophy of process in education it means that one of the tasks of the teacher is to create a milieu in which the young can often generate their own questions and explore ways in which to answer them. Slowly, we must nurture in children an ability to live with uncertainties, to understand the creative Socratic state of not knowing now in order that one may know more fully later, of being able to work with tentative scraps and engaging details until such time as they form new unities of insight, perception and feeling. The teacher's task is to cultivate the art of thinking within existence, of re-creating within existence and of refining within existence. He is committed to developing a fidelity to experience and the crystallization of experience through symbolic forms. In *The Dawn of Day* Nietzsche eloquently described the state of happy expectancy which would be the hallmark of an education dedicated to the concept of process:

> Everything is veiled, in suspense; we know nothing of what is going on, but simply wait and try to be *prepared*. At the same time we experience a pure and purifying feeling of profound irresponsibility, rather like that felt by a spectator before a drawn curtain – *it* is growing, *it* is coming to light; we have nothing to do with determining its value, or the hour of its arrival. We are thrown back altogether upon indirect, beneficient and defensive influences. 'Something greater than we are is growing here' – such is our most secret hope: we prepare everything with a view to its most auspicious entry into the world – not only everything useful, but the noblest gifts of our souls. So sacredly should we live – can we live! Whether what we are expecting is a thought or a deed, our relationship to every essential achievement is none other than that of pregnancy, and all our vain-glorious talk of 'willing' and 'creating' should be cast to the winds. This is the true *ideal selfishness*: always to watch over and possess the soul in patience that our productivity may *come to a beautiful termination*! . . . [87]

Following the Existentialist tradition, I have tended to discuss education in terms of individuals and creative process. Yet, following in the wake of Martin Buber's philosophy, I suspect, paradoxically, this can only be realized through the power of relationships and the power of community. The school as an institution cannot be separated from the school as the place where a true form of education takes place. It is only consistent, then, that *the school itself* should become a living and dynamic experiment. The life of the school with all its diversities and contrasts should also be seen as the raw material to be shaped, refined, developed.

'Without contraries is no progression', wrote William Blake, and it is an aphorism which, as we have seen, the Existentialists, from Heraclitus forwards, would endorse – yet how many schools could be said to apply the wisdom locked in the proverb? What institutions dare allow the intellectual conflicts that simmer between their members to boil in order that there might be spiritual progress? Which institution has the courage and conviction to see its own relationships, its own unities and disunities, its whole tangled network of perspectives, ambitions, insights, theories, emotions, fantasies, as *the primary material* of the educational process? Institutions tend to smother the differences between their members in order to manufacture an administrative cohesion, and in this way secure the external tasks (certification, of some sort, for 95% of their members) they have set themselves. This is understandable. But if we define education as expressive activity, as *the continuous process through which we give shape to life itself*, then the educational institution must in turn be seen as clay to be shaped according to the evolving conceptions of all its members. Indeed, the social form of a school should, properly, emerge out of its own teaching, out of the sustained collaborative difficult discussion of what is seen to be most fundamental to life. Such discussion can only take place effectively in relatively small schools – and it has been the master-stroke of political parties during the last two decades to make schools so large that they could only ever become, at best, diffuse and benevolent bureaucracies. If individuality and community are complementary concepts, then we cannot have a full education for the child until we have secured a sense of true community in our schools.

Theodore Roethke, the American poet, once declared, 'When I create I am true and would like to find the strength to base my life entirely on this truth, and on this infinite simplicity and joy'. Other poets might want to modify such a remark, but I think most would want to accept the existential intention it embodies – namely, the desire to extend the creative process beyond the specific artefact (in which it culminated) to life itself. The Existentialists would have us see education as pre-eminently concerned with process rather than with product, with that process in which we try to understand and shape our ever-precarious lives. George Grant*, in his valuable book on Nietzsche, *Time as History*, summarizing the philosopher's challenge, wrote:

> Therefore the question for our species is: can we reach a new height which takes into itself not only the ecstasy of a noble encounter with chaos, but also the results of the long history of rationalism? Neither the nihilists nor the last men deserve to be masters of the earth. The nihilists only go on willing for the sake of willing. They assuage their restlessness by involvement in mastery for its own sake. They are unable to use their mastery for joy. The last men simply use the fruits of technique for the bored pursuit of their trivial vision

*I should point out that George Grant himself does not share Nietzsche's view.

> of happiness. The question is whether there can be men who transcend the alternatives of being nihilists or last men; who know that they are the creators of their own values, but bring forth from that creation in the face of chaos a joy in their willing which will make them deserving of being masters of the earth.[88]

Such a creating in the face of chaos, such a determined making, unmaking and remaking of life itself in order that there should be more life in the form of greater consciousness, lies at the heart of education conceived existentially. The task is immense, and for the Existentialist there is, and can be, no inevitability about the outcome.

SIX

On Higher Education and the Need for Intellectual and Collaborative Communities

Paideia is education looked upon as a life-long transformation of the human personality, in which every aspect of life plays a part . . . Paideia . . . is the task of giving form to the act of living itself: treating every occasion of life as a means of self-fabrication, and as part of a larger process of converting facts into values, processes into purposes, hopes and plans into consummation and realisations. Paideia is not merely a learning: it is a making and a shaping; and man himself is the work of art that paideia seeks to form.

LEWIS MUMFORD

I

The literary critic George Steiner has defined the dominant tone of intellectual discourse in England as one of 'minimalism'. England, Steiner claimed, left him with the impression 'of wilful insularity', of 'reduction', of 'a general meagreness in philosophical thinking'. The English literary tone was marked by 'an unmistakeable thinness, a sparsity, a sour fastidiousness'. As for English philosophical practice, it was little more than scholastic, and generally withdrawn from life. 'We have to recognize', wrote Steiner, 'how little it has to do with the potential of philosophy as a central informing agency in private and public action.' Steiner's picture is of a flat plateau painted in greys. And yet, I would suggest, it is a fairly accurate painting. It records, at least, what I have often felt, and is confirmed by my experience of editing the journal *Tract* over a period of six years. Again and again, I have had to conclude that the minority taking seriously the life of ideas, of culture, of consciousness and its refinement, is too small, too scattered, to support such a publication. There is something in the very climate of contemporary England hostile to serious philosophical engagement, hostile to the development of imagination and intellect alike. Everything must be expressed in a minor key and in a manner casual and almost cynical, so that the person speaking is always protected, always already half out of the fairly predictable position he has adopted – just in case some naive fool takes him seriously! Other critics of our society have pointed to the same failing, and other editors like Ian Robinson, editor of the now defunct *Human World*, suffered from the same intellectual bleakness. It can be partly, but only partly, understood as the condition we have inherited from three long decades of arid Positivism. The Oxford philosophers *were* rather successful in destroying the rich indigenous life of the human mind and in making the extraordinary seem rather ordinary and the ordinary rather pointless.

If we look at education, as I did in the opening essay of this book, we find a similar drabness. Indeed, it is rather uncanny how the political Right and the political Left mirror each other. In both we find the same utilitarianism: an emphasis on the mastery of techniques and fact without any reference to informing purposes; an emphasis on skills and a deafening silence about meanings. In both there is a lamentable absence of philosophical thought, an absence of grounding principles. Or, it might be more accurate to say, there are grounding principles in educational discourse but that they are highly instrumentalist in character, concerned to fit education to the industrial system in order to secure increased 'growth' and efficiency.

It is not altogether surprising, then, that the vast majority of our educational institutions in this country seem incapable of representing any coherent body of values. What values they possess derive from the dominant demands of a technocracy which has little place for human meanings and aspirations. Our institutions quietly serve the commercial and political demands for efficiency, technical know-how, production and consumption, manipulative power. With such values, our educational institutions are impotent to create cultural and collaborative communities and powerless to create an education which not only informs but broadens and deepens human consciousness, making it a task with both a communal and a solitary dimension. On the immense cultural, moral and economic problems which confront the last quarter of our confused century our educational institutions have remained ominously blank. I hope to return later in this essay to the social responsibilities of institutions of higher education. Our colleges, polytechnics and universities, it would seem, have assiduously avoided the fundamental discussion of ends. And yet it would seem to me that any intellectual community should be constantly drawing to the front of its consciousness those uncomfortable but rewarding questions which raise the problem of meaning, value and significance. An intellectual community should be trying to draw new relationships between different forms of knowledge and creation, relationships which in turn alter and extend those original forms. This is a simple observation. But it is of crucial importance for if this sense of collaborative exchange isn't developed, then the disciplines break off from the mainland and become small islands, dangerously out of touch. Isolated study is always prone to erect a partial insight into the total explanation. With the breaking off of disciplines the two interwoven communities – the community of diverse understanding and the community of individuals – are destroyed. For these reasons it is imperative that those studying and teaching in different areas of enquiry come often together, in order to share, relate and differentiate between the different modes of intellectual and creative exploration. It is imperative, but it does not and will not happen easily. Not only does the dreary intellectual climate militate against it, but so does the very size of our amalgamated and expanding institutions (where to speak of 'communities' is, in so many cases, to misuse a vital word); so also does the crazy, anxious, market-seeking conconction of atomistic courses which make up a typical curriculum in higher places of 'learning'.

It must also be obvious that it is equally important for individuals within the intellectual community to have sustained periods of time in which they can develop their own particular contribution to intellectual and creative thought. Individuals should be out on the frontiers of their own disciplines, pressing into new territory. Here, one feels, there should develop a rich and powerful dialectic between *individual* reading/creating/researching and *communal* discussion/sounding out/teaching/performance. The intellectual community, if it is to thrive, if it is to create the proper climate for the flower of consciousness, must establish a delicate balance between these polar but complementary energies. A member of the intellectual community should be able to experience both the difficult and occasionally intoxicating pleasures of solitary creation and also the rewards of collaborative exchange. These are not totally separate activities, for each runs into the other, conferring weight, dignity and meaning. And both depend upon that sense of engaged process which I described in the last essay. If the balance is broken we discover either, on the one side, academic isolationism (as in, for example, some of the old universities) or, on the other side, a casual pseudo-intellectual gregariousness (as in some of the new). And, of course, either of these failings have an immediate and detrimental effect on teaching. For teaching cannot be isolated from the surrounding milieu in which it takes place. If an intellectual community is not forging fresh concepts and new forms of symbolic expression, if it is not drawing together for sustained collaborative exchange, if it is not drawing its materials from an existential process of discovery, then the teaching within that community will lack both depth and effervescence.

The broad challenge facing an alert intellectual community, brought together by a common concern with education and culture, could not be more momentous. It urges us to look over the walls of our own garden to establish a wider and necessary sense of the whole neighbourhood. One of the tasks confronting us is to find *principles of unity*, bold integrating concepts evolving out of intellectual and passionate discussion within and across all the major disciplines of expression and knowledge. Ernst Cassirer pointed to the exacting problem in *An Essay on Man* when he quoted Max Scheler:

> In no other period of human knowledge has man ever become more problematic to himself than in our own days. We have a scientific, a philosophical, and a theological anthropology that know nothing of each other. Therefore we no longer possess any clear and consistent idea of man. The ever-growing multiplicity of the particular sciences that are engaged in the study of men has much more confused and obscured than elucidated our concept of man.[89]

According to Cassirer, we have amassed an astoundingly rich body of materials, an abundance of methodologies, but failed to draw them together into any comprehensive relationship. The outcome of such an abundance has, paradoxically, led to the dire poverty of specialism which has in turn created an 'educated' people divided among itself and deprived of a common language through which it can easily share its experience. Ironically, the outcome of intellectual abundance has been the general meagreness and paucity to which a number of critics have drawn our attention, and to which I alluded at the beginning of this essay. Cassirer concluded the opening chapter (entitled 'The Crisis in Man's Knowledge of Himself') of the book referred to above, as follows:

> When compared with our own abundance the past may seem very poor. But our wealth of facts is not necessarily a wealth of thoughts. Unless we succeed in finding a clue of Ariadne to lead us out of this labyrinth, we can have no real insight into the general character of human culture; we shall remain lost in a mass of disconnected and disintegrated data which seem to lack all conceptual unity.[90]

I am claiming that one of the critical tasks of the intellectual community is to attempt to articulate a dynamic and coherent concept of man. Such a concept cannot be wholly enunciated in advance, but it will inevitably be made up of many insights, shafts of understanding, tested knowledge, emerging knowledge, speculation, embodied expression developed in different ways (by individuals working alone or in small groups, by individuals working within the disciplines and across them and, perhaps, even outside them) and brought together. Of course, it must be granted that unity cannot be mechanically imposed and that disunity, organically arrived at, is infinitely more desirable. But then disunity, dialectically conceived, can be a prelude to a more complex higher unity, containing and transcending the previous differences. Put another way, I am suggesting that there is an urgent need for a broad, generous and open phenomenological examination of symbolic forms. This might take many shapes, but one way would be for the intellectual community to come together to examine industrial culture in all its ramifications.* Such an interdisciplinary study of our own complex culture – with its various strengths and its harsh pathologies – would be demanding in the extreme, but invaluable; and never more needed than now in the strange twilight of our Western world. Such a study should surely become, as I suggested in an earlier essay, a major interdisciplinary degree

*Another study which needs making, and which colleges of education and education departments would be uniquely equipped to make, is the collaborative elucidation of types of knowing. These types of knowing could be related to the various disciplines, and an attempt made to create a balanced curriculum. At the moment, as I have stressed throughout this book, the expressive disciplines in which, for example, one *knows* about a state of consciousness by embodying it in symbolic form, are severely neglected. In brief, the theory of symbolic forms needs sympathetic but critical examination; it then needs to be related to the curriculum.

course. It would cut across all the traditional boundaries and would demand the charting of a new intellectual map: a map that would inevitably have unpredictable but explosive consequences for society.

Such work is urgent because of the danger constituted by the disintegration of knowledge into atomistic fragments. It is urgent also because of the mundane level of consciousness in the surrounding society, a society encouraged at every point by the mass-communications industry to become 'preoccupied with becoming unpreoccupied'. The latter observation brings me to a point which was implicit in my opening essay. In the Herculean task of existentially exploring and collaboratively relating meanings, concepts and symbolic creations the intellectual community would inevitably become a critical energy within the society of which it is an ambiguous member. The intellectual community would urge society to interpret its own conditions by injecting illuminating concepts into the dark data of human experience, and also by creating art which illuminated man's true condition. It would encourage a problematic and dual awareness, an awareness both of what is and also of what might be. It would promote such awareness, not through political revolution, not through bureaucratic manipulation, not through the manufacturing of mindless slogans, but simply by introducing symbols and conceptions, alternative forms of structuring, relating and evaluating experience. The intellectual community symbolizes the power of consciousness and the power of imagination, in the ordering and reordering of life. Certainly, in visiting schools, I have observed how the more lively teachers look to the higher institutes of education for intellectual and creative sustenance. They look to them as to enclaves wherein they hope to find a freer play of mind over experience than is at present allowed in schools, places where the social and individual events of our confused age can be evaluated at a level above the dreary ad hoc opportunisms of politicians, bureaucrats, media pundits and money-makers. The paucity of intellectual and imaginative life in England today dialectically points us to the primary task of education, particularly at its higher levels. Nor at such a critical stage should we cultivate false modesty and practise the evasive arts of self-diminution. We must insist on the formative power of ideas and of true culture in the world of action and reflection alike.

I have tried in this essay to establish the need for such a sharing of discourse and to suggest its most appropriate shape. If, in the current demands for efficiency and utility, the institutes of higher education fail to create, first within themselves and then within our society, an awareness of the need for generative principles and expressive symbolism – the need, in brief, for the continuous culture of the mind and the feelings – then they will have betrayed one of their primary functions, and destroyed one of the main means by which society can recognize and thus, if it so willed, transcend itself. In truth, one cannot be optimistic about the education provided in our various institutions for higher education. The conditions are not conducive to profound intellectual exploration and collaboration. It would seem that the powers to administer and regulate are regarded more highly than powers to create, understand and teach. Wherever we look, we find a tendency for means to become ends, for the secondary to be illegitimately converted into the primary. We also find innumerable distracting problems generated simply by the scale of operations: the problems of fragmentation and anonymity. Charles Boyle's recent description of higher education in *The Times Higher Educational Supplement* would seem, without exaggeration, to sum up the plight of these institutions:

> Within our colleges we see bureaucracy rampant, the dominance of administrators over teachers and researchers, a continual and undignified rat-race by staff for a niche in the hierarchy, a sense of remoteness and homelessness among students. The dehumanised language of industry becomes commonplace; the 'management' talks of 'efficiency', 'output', 'input', 'cost benefit analyses', 'redundancy', as if a real effort was being made to spread the alienation of the factory floor to the lecture room.
>
> Knowledge is regarded as a commodity and the education industry is designed to 'produce' it, preferably in quantified blocks, which can be easily controlled by the bureaucrats and easily labelled as the preserves of particular specialists.[91]

Here, once again, Charles Boyle provides us with a picture of a flat plateau painted in greys. Against such a bleak landscape what can one do but assert another vision such as Graham Carey and myself gave expression to in *Proposal for a New College*, a college built on new foundations, on existential, cultural and ecological principles? The proposal has been dismissed as impossibly utopian. Yet it is only through an ideal that one can move beyond the present, and it is only by striving for the impossible that one can incarnate more of the possible. What cannot be doubted is that a number of individuals, committed to the life of consciousness, are now seriously considering the need for an alternative pattern of education, perhaps a cluster of differentiated small autonomous colleges in which education as that passionate enquiry into meaning through all the symbolic forms of cognition and expression, and predicated on true relationships, can begin again. Such a fragile event is yet a sign of change and growth, from which, perhaps, a richer future will unfurl. Such experiments in education have now become essential. Outside these experiments, individuals in higher education, committed to the intellectual and collaborative community, may have no choice but to draw together and work somewhat subversively, somewhat precariously, in the interstices of the vast and unwieldly structures of state education.

References

1 Robert Witkin: *The Intelligence of Feeling* (Heinemann Educational Books).
2 George Orwell: *1984* (Penguin).
3 David Jones, quoted by Kathleen Raine in *David Jones and the Actually Loved and Known* (Golgonooza Press).
4 The Green Paper *Education in Our Schools* 1977 (HMSO).
5 Ibid.
6 Ibid.
7 Robert Cushman: Preface to *Therapeia* (Greenwood Press).
8 Quoted in James Hillman's *Emotion* (Routledge and Kegan Paul).
9 Ibid.
10 Ibid.
11 Ibid.
12 Ibid.
13 Aristotle: *Ethics* (Penguin).
14 Plato: *Phaedrus* (Penguin).
15 R. S. Peters: *Psychology and Ethical Development* (Unwin University Books).
16 Sandra, in unpublished ms, *What I Truly Feel*, introduced by Bernard Harrison.
17 Ibid.
18 Laban: *A Life for Dance* (Macdonald and Evans).
19 D. H. Lawrence in *Preface to New Poems: Selected Essays* (Penguin).
20 Quoted in Susanne Langer's *Mind: An Essay on Human Feeling* (Johns Hopkins Press).
21 Poem by Janette Brookes quoted in Peter Abbs' *English for Diversity* (Heinemann Educational Books).
22 Ernst Cassirer: *The Philosophy of Symbolic Forms* (Yale University Press).
23 From a piece of autobiography written by a student, as part of an undergraduate course at the University of Sussex.
24 Descartes: *A Discourse on Method*, translated by John Veitch (Everyman).
25 Ibid.
26 Pascal: *Pensées*, translated by Morris Bishop (Dell).
27 Ibid.
28 Marjorie Grene: *The Knower and the Known* (Faber).
29 John Locke: *An Essay Concerning Human Understanding* (Everyman).
30 John Stuart Mill: *Mill on Bentham and Coleridge*, ed. F. R. Leavis (Chatto & Windus).

31 John Stuart Mill: *Autobiography* (Signet).
32 David Hume, quoted in Lewis Mumford's *The Pentagon of Power* (Secker and Warburg).
33 Plato: *Republic* Book III. Jowett's translation.
34 R. C. Lodge, quoted in Herbert Read's *Ikon and Idea* (Faber).
35 Susanne Langer: *Philosophy in a New Key* (Harvard University Press).
36 Ibid.
37 Laban: *A Life for Dance* (Macdonald and Evans).
38 Edward Carpenter: *Eskimo Realities* (Holt, Rinehart & Winston).
39 Edward Sapir: *Culture, Language and Personality* (University of California Press).
40 Ernst Cassirer: *An Essay on Man* (Mentor).
41 Edward Sapir, op. cit.
42 Shelley: *Defense of Poetry.*
43 Neitzsche: *The Portable Nietzsche*, ed. Walter Kaufmann (The Viking Press).
44 Goethe, quoted in Harold Bloom's *The Anxiety of Influence* (Oxford University Press).
45 From *The Observer*, 9 May 1976.
46 Northrop Frye: *The Modern Century* (Oxford University Press).
47 Ron Goulart: *The Assault on Childhood* (Gollancz).
48 From a letter in the *Radio Times.*
49 Jules Henry: *Culture Against Man* (Penguin).
50 Quoted in *Entertainment and Exploitation* by Joanna Nash (Responsible Society).
51 *The Observer*, 9 May 1976.
52 Seymour Betsky: *Towards a Critique of Industrial Culture: Tract 15* (Gryphon Press).
53 Taken from blurb for *Chopper* (New English Library).
54 Peggie Harper, quoted in *Radio Times* 29 November 1975.
55 Stanley Diamond: *The Primitive and the Civilised: Tract 18* (Gryphon Press).
56 Report on Dr Belson's research: *The Guardian*, 7 September 1977.
57 Uri Bronfennbrenner: *Two Worlds of Childhood* (Allen & Unwin).
58 Ibid.
59 Kierkegaard: *The Point of View*, translated by Lowrie (Oxford University Press).
60 Ibid.
61 Ibid.
62 Dostoevsky: *Notes From the Underground.*
63 St Augustine: *Autobiography*, translated by Sheed (Sheed & Ward).
64 Martin Buber: *Between Man and Man* (Fontana).
65 Heraclitus: 'Fragments', listed in *Early Greek Philosophy* by J. Burnet (Black).
66 Ibid.
67 Ortega y Gasset: *The Origin of Philosophy* (Norton).
68 Heraclitus, op. cit.
69 Ibid.
70 Ibid.
71 Ibid.
72 Ibid.

73 Ibid.
74 Ibid.
75 Ibid.
76 Plato: *Apologia*, translated by Tredennick (Penguin).
77 Ibid.
78 Pascal: *Notes for a Preface to a Treatise on Geometry or on Logic*, translated by Morris Bishop (Dell).
79 Marx and Engels: quoted in *The Ethics of Reason* by F. A. Lea (Brentham Press).
80 Nietzsche: *Beyond Good and Evil*, translated by Hollingdale (Penguin).
81 Kierkegaard: quoted in *Kierkegaard*, introduced by W. H. Auden (Cassell).
82 Darwin: *Autobiography* (Collins).
83 Einstein, quoted in Arthur Koestler's *The Act of Creation* (Picador).
84 Liam Hudson: *The Cult of the Fact* (Cape).
85 D. H. Lawrence: *Collected Letters* (Heinemann).
86 W. B. Yeats: 'The Circus Animals' Desertion', in *Collected Poems* (Macmillan).
87 Nietzsche: *The Dawn of Day*, quoted in Frank Lea's *The Tragic Philosopher* (Methuen).
88 George Grant: *Time as History* (Canadian Broadcasting Corporation).
89 Max Scheler, quoted in Ernst Cassirer's *Essay on Man* (Mentor).
90 Ernst Cassirer: *Essay on Man* (Mentor).
91 Charles Boyle, quoted in *The Times Higher Educational Supplement*, June 30 1978.

Index

Note: Many entries have several references per page. For items not in index please consult References, pp. 129-31.